THE IRISH B & B COOKBOOK

THE IRISH B & B COOKBOOK

ANN MULLIGAN

Mercier Press
Cork
www.mercierpress.ie

Trade enquiries to CMD Distribution
55A Spruce Avenue, Stillorgan Industrial Park, Blackrock, County Dublin.

ISBN: 978 1 85635 583 4

10 9 8 7 6 5 4 3 2 1

A CIP record for this title is available from the British Library

Mercier Press receives financial assistance from the Arts Council / An Comhairle Ealaíon

Printed and bound by J.H. Haynes & Co. Ltd, Sparkford.

Contents

Measurements:

Mililitres	Fluid ounces	Ounces	Grams
5ml	¼ fluid oz	¼oz	5g
15ml	½ fluid oz	½oz	15g
25ml	1fluid oz	1oz	28g
50ml	2 fluid oz	2oz	55g
75ml	3 fluid oz	3oz	85g
100ml	4 fluid oz	4oz	115g
125ml	5 fluid oz	5oz	140g
150ml	6 fluid oz	6oz	170g
175ml	7 fluid oz	7oz	200g
200ml	8 fluid oz	8oz	225g
250ml	10 fluid oz	10oz	285g
300ml	12 fluid oz	12oz	340g
350ml	14 fluid oz	14oz	400g
400ml	16 fluid oz	16oz	455g
800ml	32 fluid oz	32oz	900g

A note on American cups:

The following tables give some basic conversions to American cups:

Wet cups:

Mililitres	Wet Cups
55ml	¼ cup
110ml	½ cup
220ml	1 cup
440ml	2 cups

Dry cups:

Grams	Cups
40g	¼ cup
75g	½ cup
150g	1 cup
300g	2 cups

Foreword

All the best ideas are the most obvious and who better to do a B&B Cookbook than Ann Mulligan who has in just a few short years built up a loyal clientele, a host of admirers and a string of awards for An Bohreen, the charming B&B she runs with her husband Jim.

This book is the result of two years' hard work where Ann shares her repertoire of recipes which have been so enjoyed and much requested by her guests.

The collection is an eclectic mix of traditional and contemporary, a microcosm of Irish food today; no mixes, packages or artificial ingredients in Ann's pantry. All the recipes are based on beautiful fresh produce. The techniques are simple because Ann really wants others to be able to reproduce and enjoy the flavours of An Bohreen – a delicious collection.

Darina Allen

Introduction

Living in Ireland and owning a B&B is a dream come true. My joy comes from presenting a guest with a meal that brings them back time after time. I have received countless requests for my recipes, which prompted me to write this book. I have included all of these favourites and hope you can enjoy them at home with fond memories of your time spent at An Bohreen.

Cooking has always been a creative outlet for me. I began at age eight, making scrambled eggs for my baby brothers. Watching them gobble up my creation, I was hooked. My father worked as a chef for many years and my maternal grandmother was well known for skills in the kitchen. My mother was an especially good baker, and allowed me to be her extra hands in the kitchen. By age ten I was making jams, preserving fruit and vegetables, as well as cooking dinner.

As a tourist I discovered Ballymaloe Cookery School, and dreamed of someday attending. My dream came true in January 2000. Working with the freshest ingredients, proper equipment and trained instructors was the most fantastic experience I could imagine. Learning to appreciate fresh flavours and value seasonal produce was indeed a prized lesson. I would like to pass this on to everyone that uses this book.

Quality and taste are key priorities in my cooking. I use fresh local ingredients, purchasing organic produce whenever possible. I do not advocate using artificial flavours or processed foods. I prefer flavours that are real and, therefore, identifiable to the person eating them. People travel from all over the world to enjoy our Irish food. Our quality seafood, lamb, beef and dairy products are widely appreciated.

Having these ingredients within our grasp I cannot understand anyone not using them at every opportunity. Recipes are only as good as their ingredients and we have a wealth of fabulous ingredients available in this country.

Cooking seasonal food is essential for flavour. No amount of spicing or splashing with sauces can replace fresh taste. I have included a variety of recipes that can be made throughout the year. My little neighbour told me fish and chips always taste better on sunny days, while stew is better on rainy days. If a child can reason this, I feel it is simple enough for an adult to understand. Somewhere a marketing executive is cringing.

Included in this book are recipes handed down from my grandmother and mother. I share them with you as a dedication to their strength and love. Passing on their legacy is something I hope you will do as well. Your family deserves to share the memories you create. Do not be intimidated by any of my recipes – to me *every* recipe is a creation. Watching my family and friends enjoy my food is such a great feeling. I want you to feel this joy too.

Bon Appetit!

Ann Mulligan

Breakfast Favourites

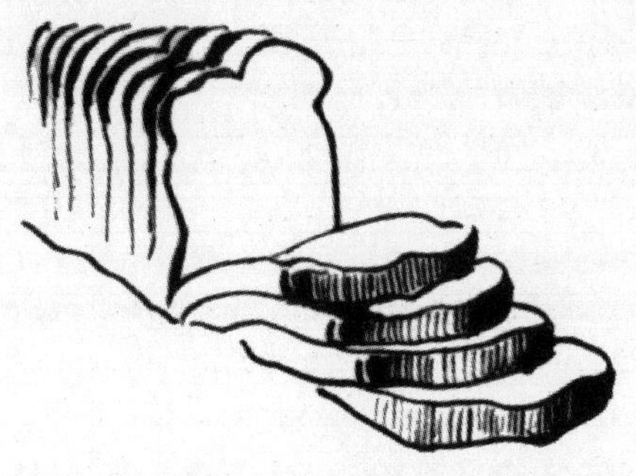

Waffles with Crispy Bacon & Pecans

Serves 8

285g / 10oz strong white flour
1½ tbsps caster sugar
1 tbsp baking powder
½ tsp salt
4 streaky rashers
50g / 2oz pecans
2 eggs, separated
350ml / 14 fluid oz milk
75ml / 3 fluid oz sunflower oil

Method:

1. Heat the waffle iron (essential for this recipe).
2. Combine the flour, sugar, baking powder, and salt in a large mixing bowl and set aside.
3. Fry the streaky rashers in a frying pan until they are crisp. Drain on a paper towel, crumble and set them aside.
4. Toast the pecans in a small sauté pan or in a hot oven until they are fragrant and just beginning to brown. Remove to a chopping board, cool and then finely chop them. Add nuts to the crumbled streaky rashers.
5. Combine the egg yolks, milk, and oil in a measuring jug. Pour into the flour mixture and stir to combine. Add the crumbled rashers and nuts.
6. Beat the egg whites until they are stiff. Fold into the batter, evenly distributing until mixed in.
7. Cook the waffle-mix in the waffle iron according to manufacturer's instructions. Keep them warm in an oven until the desired quantity is made. Serve with butter and some warmed maple syrup.

An Bohreen Frittata

Serves 8
Preheat oven to 200C (400F)

55g / 2oz streaky rashers,
cut into ¼-inch dice
115g / 4oz black pudding, crumbled
115g / 4oz diced mild onion
85g / 3oz diced green bell pepper
85g / 3oz diced red bell pepper
1 clove garlic, minced
225g / 8oz cubed peeled potatoes
115g / 4oz diced mushrooms
10 eggs
150ml / 6 fluid oz sour cream
225g / 8oz grated cheddar cheese
115g / 4oz grated Parmesan cheese
½ tsp dried basil
1 tsp dried oregano
½ tsp dried parsley
Pinch of cayenne pepper
¼ tsp salt
½ tsp black pepper
28g / 1oz butter
55g / 2oz grated Parmesan for garnish

Method:

1. Cook the diced rasher in a frying pan until crisp. Reserve the dripping in the pan and sauté the onions, mushrooms, bell peppers, and garlic. Transfer to a bowl and set aside. Add the potatoes to the skillet and sauté until they are just tender when pierced with a skewer. Combine with the other vegetables in a bowl.

2. Beat the eggs in a medium-sized bowl; add the sour cream, cheeses, herbs, and seasonings. Pour this into vegetable mixture. Add the streaky rasher and black pudding. Stir to combine.
3. Melt the butter in a 12-inch non-stick, ovenproof frying pan. Pour in the frittata mixture and cook over a medium heat until the edges are set and the centre is not fully cooked. Place into an oven at 200C (400F) for 10 to 15 minutes.The centre will complete cooking in oven.
4. Cut into wedges, sprinkle with some Parmesan and serve.

An Bohreen Nut Granola

Makes about 1350g / 50oz
Preheat oven to 180C (350F)

300ml / 12 fluid oz honey
200ml / 8 fluid oz sunflower oil
455g / 16oz oat flakes
200g / 7oz barley flakes
200g / 7oz wheat flakes
115g / 4oz rye flakes
140g / 5oz raisins
140g / 5oz toasted and chopped hazelnuts
225g / 8oz toasted sunflower seeds
225g / 8oz toasted pumpkin seeds
55g / 2oz chopped dried apricots
115g / 4oz chopped dates
115g / 4oz of either pecans or walnuts (I use both) toasted
225g / 8oz combination dried cranberries, dried blueberries, dried cherries

Method:

1. Combine the honey and oil in a small saucepan – warm just enough to melt the honey. Whisk the honey and oil together.
2. Combine the flakes in a large bowl. Pour the honey-oil onto the flakes and stir well to mix.
3. Spread the flakes onto 2 or 3 baking sheets. Bake in an oven at 180C (350F) for 20 to 30 minutes, stirring frequently. Toast the grains but do not roast the grains. Cool, stirring frequently to evenly mix the grains. When cool add the fruit and nuts. Store in airtight container.

Makes a lovely addition to biscuits and gives a nice crunch. Simply add when mixing dry ingredients for your favourite biscuit recipe.

Breakfast Home Fries

Serves 2

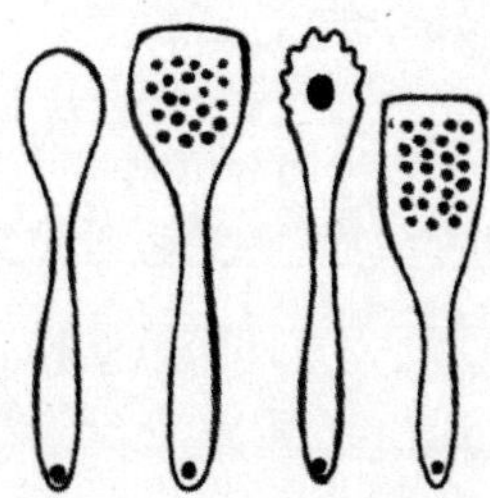

2 medium rooster potatoes, unpeeled
1 small Granny Smith apple
1 leek, white part only
3 mushrooms, chopped
¼ red bell pepper
Pinch of thyme leaves
Salt and pepper
1–2 tbsps butter

Method:

1. Boil the potatoes whole and unpeeled for 8 minutes. Drain and plunge the potatoes into cold water to stop the cooking process. Peel and cut into ½-inch dice.
2. Peel, core, and dice the apple, mushrooms, and red pepper. Chop leek into similar size.
3. Melt the butter in a frying pan, and add the vegetables and apple. Sauté until tender, then season with thyme, salt and pepper. Keep in warmed oven until needed.

Serve with chicken livers on toast or Irish rarebit.

Buckwheat Pancakes

Serves 4

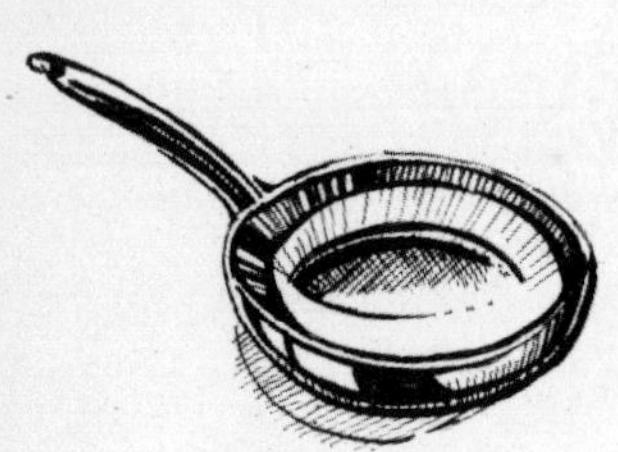

85g / 3oz buckwheat flour
85g / 3oz strong white flour
½ tsp salt
1 tbsp caster sugar
¼ tsp cream of tartar
2 tsps baking powder
1 egg, beaten
200ml / 8 fluid oz milk
28g / 1oz butter, melted and cooled

Method:

1. Combine all of the dry ingredients in a large mixing bowl. Make a well in centre.
2. Combine the milk, egg, and butter in a mixing jug. Whisk to combine. Pour into the flour mixture and mix just until combined. If the batter seems too thick, add 50ml / 2 fluid oz more milk.
3. Heat a non-stick frying-pan over medium heat until a drop of water dances when poured onto the pan. Add a couple of drops of sunflower oil and pour in 55g / 2oz batter for each pancake. Cook until bubbles appear on top, then gently turn over and cook until they are golden brown. Remove to a plate and keep warm in an oven until the desired quantity is cooked.

Serve with some maple syrup, fresh berries or Yummy Berry Sauce (see page 25).

Yummy Berry Sauce

455g / 16oz mixed berries,
fresh or frozen
55g / 2oz blackberry jam
2 tbsps cassis or Grand Marnier
2 tsps corn flour, mixed with
2 tsps cold water

Method:

1. Place the berries in a saucepan with the jam and stir over a low heat until the jam dissolves.
2. Add the liqueur and corn flour mixture. Bring to the boil, then turn down the heat and simmer for 10 minutes.

This sauce is a staple at An Bohreen. I always keep some ready-made in the freezer for those unexpected times when a little something extra is needed. Delicious as a garnish for desserts or sauce for ice cream.

Cashel Blue Cheese Strata

Serves 4–6
Preheat oven to 170C (325F)

340g / 12oz Cashel Blue cheese
340g / 12oz cream cheese
55g / 2oz grated Parmesan cheese
1 tbsp butter, soft
500ml / 20 fluid oz milk
50ml / 2 fluid oz dry white wine
6 eggs
455g / 16oz of ½-inch cubed ham
225g / 8oz thinly sliced mushrooms
2 scallions, thinly sliced
Dash of Tabasco sauce
½ tsp black pepper
340g / 12oz white bread, crust removed and cut into 1-inch cubes

Method:

1. Butter a 12x8x2-inch casserole dish and dust with Parmesan cheese.
2. Combine the cubed bread, diced ham, mushrooms and scallions in a mixing bowl. Toss together to evenly distribute the ingredients. Pour into a prepared casserole dish.
3. Combine the milk, wine, eggs, Cashel Blue, cream cheese, Tabasco and pepper, using a whisk or mixer. Pour over the bread mixture. Press down lightly with a spatula to allow the bread to absorb the liquids. Cover the dish with some cling film and refrigerate overnight.
4. Bring to room temperature, and bake uncovered at 170C

(325F) for 55 minutes. You'll know it is baked when a knife inserted in the centre comes out clean.

5. Cut into squares and serve with some grilled tomato or melon wedges.

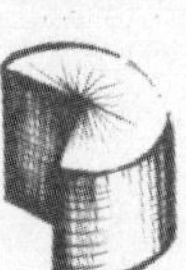

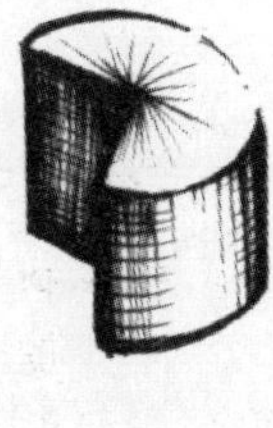

Cashel Blue & Black Pudding Tart

Serves 6–8
Preheat oven to 190C (375F)

Tart pastry

225g / 8oz strong white flour
½ tsp salt
2 tbsps caster sugar
225g / 8oz cold butter, cut into 1-inch cubes

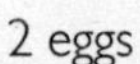

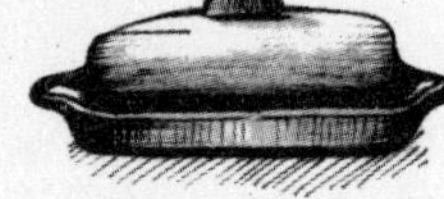

2 eggs
25ml / 1 fluid oz cold water

Pastry method:

Combine the flour, salt, and sugar in a food processor. With the motor running pulse in the butter a piece at a time, until the mixture resembles coarse crumbs. Add the eggs and water and process just until the mixture forms a ball. Flatten dough into a disc and wrap in cling film. Chill for 30 minutes.

Filling

4 tbsps butter
2 large sweet onions, sliced very thin
1 Granny Smith apple, diced
4 eggs
200ml / 8 fluid oz cream
170g / 6oz Cashel Blue cheese, crumbled
½ tsp Dijon mustard
85g / 3oz black pudding, crumbled (preferably traditional)

Filling method:

1. Melt the butter in a heavy-bottomed sauté pan. Sauté the onions over a medium-low heat until caramelised (25–35 minutes). Add the apple and sauté until it softens. Remove the mixture from the heat and let it cool. Combine the eggs, cream, and mustard in a small bowl. Whisk to combine and set aside.
2. Remove the pastry from the refrigerator and bring to room temperature. Roll out the pastry between 2 sheets of cling film. Line a 9-inch removable bottom tart pan with pastry. Trim the edges and chill for 60 minutes.
3. Cover the chilled pastry with a circle of parchment or foil cut larger than the tart. Fill it with uncooked rice or uncooked beans. Bake for 10 minutes. Remove from the oven, remove the paper and rice and allow to cool for 10 minutes. (This process is known as blind-baking). Sprinkle the pastry with onions, apple, cheese, and black pudding. Slowly pour the egg mixture into a filled tart shell. Bake for 25–30 minutes or until the tart is lightly browned and the centre is set. To test, insert a knife blade into the centre; if the blade comes out clean but moist, the tart is done. If necessary bake for a few minutes more. Remove from the oven and allow it to rest for 10 minutes before cutting.

Garnish with a fresh sprig of parsley or a small wedge of apple.

Save rice or beans for future blind-baking needs in jar marked 'blind-baking weights'.

Cheese Blintzes with Apple Sauce

Serves 4

Batter for blintz

140g / 5oz flour
Pinch of salt
75–100ml / 3–4 fluid oz milk
40g / 1½oz butter, melted
3 eggs

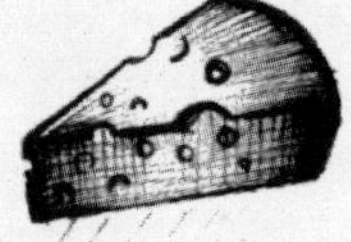

Cheese filling

455g / 16oz cottage cheese
1 egg, beaten
¼ tsp cinnamon
55g / 2oz caster sugar
Pinch of salt
½ tsp lemon zest, finely grated
½ tsp pure vanilla extract

Apple Sauce

455g / 16oz cooking apples, peeled, cored and chopped
55g / 2oz sugar or to taste
¼ tsp cinnamon
1 tbsp water

Method:

1. Place all of the ingredients for the cheese filling into a food processor or blender and process until smooth. Keep in a refrigerator until needed.
2. Place the apples, sugar, cinnamon, and water into a saucepan.

Cover with a lid and cook on low temperature until the apples cook into sauce consistency. Check to prevent sticking. Chill until needed.

3. Place the flour and salt into a food processor. Combine the egg, milk, and butter in a mixing jug, then pour into a processor with the motor running and process until the mixture is smooth.
4. Heat a crepe pan over medium heat, and then brush with a few drops of oil. Pour 55g / 2oz of the batter into the pan (or enough to cover the bottom). Tilt the pan to evenly distribute the batter. When the blintz looks solid and pulls away from the edges of the pan (blintz will not be totally cooked, just solid enough to handle), turn it out onto parchment. Place 1 tbsp of the cheese filling in the centre and fold over the opposite sides, repeat with the other two sides. The blintz should look like a rectangular envelope. Set them aside, cover with damp tea towel, repeat cooking process – the batter mixture should yield 8 blintzes.
5. To complete cooking – heat 150ml / 6 fluid oz of oil in a deep-sided pan, oil should cover blintzes and fry them until they are golden brown. Drain the blintzes on kitchen paper and serve with apple sauce on the side.

Two blintzes equals one serving. Dust with icing sugar just before serving.

Cheese & Shrimp Quiche

Serves 4–6
Preheat oven to 180C (350F)

5 slices streaky rasher
225g / 8oz mushrooms, sliced
1 scallion, chopped
85g / 3oz Emmental cheese, grated
125g / 4½oz diced cooked shrimp*
5 eggs, beaten
175ml / 7 fluid oz cream
Pinch of ground nutmeg
¼ tsp pepper
1 9-inch shortcrust pastry case, unbaked

Method:

1. Dice the rasher into ¼-inch pieces, then cook in a frying pan until crispy. Remove the rasher from the frying pan and drain on kitchen paper. Reserving the oil in the frying pan, sauté the mushrooms.
2. Place the pastry into a 9-inch quiche dish. Sprinkle the bacon, mushrooms, scallion and shrimp onto the pastry. Sprinkle cheese on top.
3. Combine the eggs, cream and spices in a mixing bowl. Whisk together to combine and pour over the ingredients in the quiche dish.
4. Bake at 180C (350F) for 30–40 minutes, or until the centre is set. Test by inserting knife into centre; if blade comes out clean but not dry, quiche is done.

Serve warm with Hashbrowns Supreme (see page 39).
This dish can also be eaten at room temperature.
*Crab meat can be substituted for shrimp.

Chicken Livers on Toast

Serves 2

3 streaky rashers, cut into ¼-inch dice
40g / 1½oz butter
340g / 12oz chicken livers
28g / 1oz flour
25ml / 1 fluid oz Madeira wine
50ml / 2 fluid oz cream
2 scallions, sliced thin
¼ tsp salt
¼ tsp black pepper
2 slices freshly toasted bread

Method:

1. Fry the streaky rasher until crisp, then drain on a paper towel. Add the butter to the dripping in the frying pan.
2. Add the salt and pepper to the flour. Dredge the chicken livers in flour. Heat the frying pan over a medium heat, then add the livers and brown on both sides for 5–8 minutes. Remove from the pan and keep warm.
3. Add the Madeira, cream, and scallions to the pan. Simmer for 2 minutes, allowing the flavours to marry. Return the livers to the pan and simmer for a further 2 minutes.

Serve on toast and garnish with fresh parsley.

Eggs Florentine

Serves 4

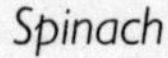

Spinach

55g / 2oz minced shallot
1 small clove garlic, minced
55g / 2oz diced streaky rasher
340g / 12oz frozen chopped
  spinach, cooked and drained
Salt to taste

Spinach method:

1. Cook streaky rasher in skillet until crispy, remove and drain. Sauté shallot and garlic until soft, add spinach and rasher, sauté for a couple of minutes and season to taste. Keep warm.

Mornay sauce

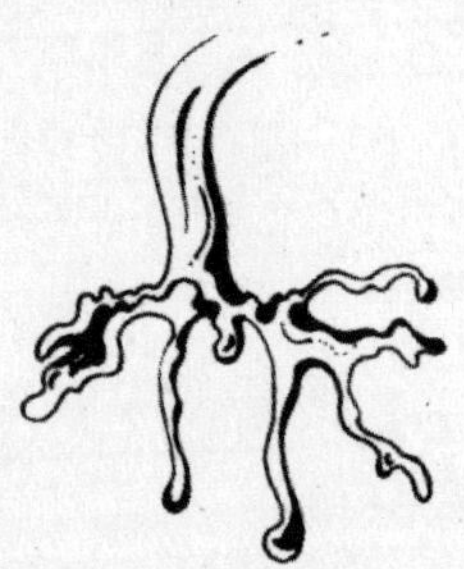

85g / 3oz butter
115g / 4oz flour
1 low-salt chicken bouillon cube
500ml / 20 fluid oz milk
100ml / 4 fluid oz cream
55g / 2oz grated Parmesan
55g / 2oz grated white aged cheddar
Salt and pepper
Pinch of nutmeg

Mornay method:

1. Melt the butter in a saucepan. Stir in the flour and cook for 10 minutes. Do not brown. Cool. Dissolve the bouillon cube in some warmed milk, then slowly add it to the flour-butter

mixture and whisk until smooth. Bring to boil and simmer for about 20 minutes. Add the cream and cheeses. Stir until smooth. Add the nutmeg, pepper and salt to taste. Be sure to taste before adding salt – cheeses add salt and you may not need any. Keep the mixture warm by placing saucepan over larger pan filled with hot water.

Eggs

8 fresh free range eggs

Eggs method:

1. Poach the eggs. Place a serving of spinach onto a warmed plate. Spoon the eggs onto the centre of the spinach nest and drizzle with the sauce.

Sprinkle with some grated nutmeg and serve immediately. Garnish with a lemon wedge.

Eggs Purgatory

Serves 4
Preheat oven to 180C (350F)

50ml / 2 fluid oz olive oil
115g / 4oz finely chopped onion
1 clove garlic, minced
2 tbsps chopped parsley
225g / 8oz minced beef
225g / 8oz pork sausage meat
455g / 16oz can of plum tomatoes
170g / 6oz tomato paste

28g / 1oz caster sugar
1 tsp salt
2 tsps dried oregano

1 tsp dried basil
Pinch of cayenne, more if desired
¼ tsp black pepper
200ml / 8 fluid oz dry red wine

4 eggs
3–4 tbsps freshly grated Parmesan cheese

Method:

1. Heat the oil in a deep pot, then sauté the onion, garlic, and herbs until the onions are soft. Add the meats and sauté until they are browned. Add the tomatoes, tomato paste, sugar, spices, herbs, and wine. Bring the mixture to boil, reduce heat, cover and simmer for 2 hours or longer if desired.
2. Heat the sauce until it starts to bubble. Put four individual ramekins or custard dishes into a roasting dish. Pour 115g / 4oz of the sauce into each dish. Place into 180C (350F)

oven and pour hot water into the roasting dish until the water comes half way up the sides of the dishes. Carefully break one egg into each dish and sprinkle with grated Parmesan cheese. Bake for 12 minutes, or until the eggs are set.

Sauce can be prepared ahead and refrigerated until needed, or frozen for future use. Serve with toasted bread for dipping.

Autumn Fruit Bowl

Serves 4–6

2 Gala, Braeburn or Granny Smith apples, cut into dice, peel if desired
28g / 1oz walnuts, toasted and coarsely chopped
115g / 4oz fresh blueberries
225g / 8oz red seedless grapes
340g / 12oz can mandarin oranges, drained

Fruit method:

Combine in a large bowl and set aside.

Dressing

225g / 8oz cream cheese, room temperature

2 tbsps of Irish honey

2 tbsps of fresh lemon juice
2 tbsps of Grand Marnier or brandy

Dressing method:

Place all of the ingredients in a mixing bowl. Whisk until the mixture is creamy, and pour it over the fruit just before serving.

Garnish with mint leaves.

Hashbrowns Supreme

Serves 6
Preheat oven to 190C (375F)

3–4 medium size potatoes, unpeeled
6 streaky rashers
55g / 2oz chopped scallions
55g / 2oz chopped red bell pepper
250ml / 10 fluid oz can of cream
of mushroom soup
50ml / 2 fluid oz sour cream
50ml / 2 fluid oz dry white wine
2 tsps horseradish cream
55g / 2oz grated sharp cheddar cheese

Method:

1. Bring a large saucepan of water to boil. Drop in the potatoes and boil for 8 minutes. Drain, and set aside to cool. When cool enough to handle, peel and coarsely grate. Measure should equal 455g / 16oz. Freeze any leftovers for future use.
2. Butter a 10x6x2-inch baking dish. Spread the grated potatoes to evenly cover the bottom of the dish.
3. Cook the streaky rashers in a skillet until crisp. Drain the rashers on a paper towel and crumble. Set aside. Sauté the scallions and red pepper in a frying pan with the dripping. When tender remove them from the heat and set aside.
4. Combine the mushroom soup, wine, sour cream, and horseradish in a mixing bowl. Stir in the pepper–scallion mixture. Pour over the potatoes and spread evenly with a spatula. Sprinkle with the crumbled bacon. *Can be prepared to this point, covered and refrigerated until ready to bake. Bring to room temperature before baking.*

5. Bake at 190C (375F) for 30 minutes. Remove from the oven and sprinkle the grated cheese over the top, return to oven and bake for 5–10 minutes or until the cheese melts. Cut into squares and serve with eggs cooked in any desired way.

Irish Rarebit

Serves 3–4

455g / 16oz aged Irish cheddar cheese
1 tbsp butter
200ml / 8 fluid oz Murphy's stout,
or a pale stout of your choice
½ tsp dry mustard powder
1 tsp Worcestershire sauce
Pinch of cayenne
2 vine ripe tomatoes
Brown bread, sliced and toasted

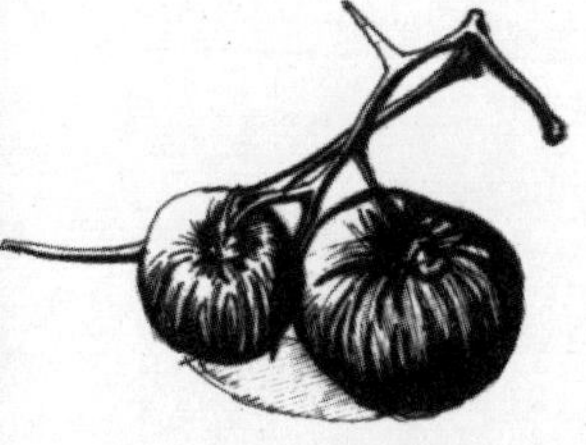

Method:

1. Grate the cheese.
2. Over a low heat melt the butter in the top of a *bain-marie* or double boiler. Add the cheese, constantly stirring with a wooden spoon. As the cheese begins to melt, slowly add the stout. Again, stir constantly to obtain a creamy texture. Add the dry mustard, Worcestershire, and cayenne. Remove from the heat and keep warm.
3. Toast the bread, place some tomato slices onto it and spoon the cheese sauce over the top. Garnish with finely minced chives or parsley.

If *bain-marie* or double boiler is not available place a glass bowl over pan of boiling water and proceed. Do not allow bottom of bowl to touch hot water, or mixture will cook, not melt.

Maui French Toast

Serves 4

6 eggs, beaten
55g / 2oz caster sugar
50ml / 2 fluid oz Grand Marnier liqueur
200ml / 8 fluid oz cream
1 tsp pure vanilla extract
55g / 2oz butter
25ml / 1 fluid oz sunflower oil
1-day-old French bread
Granulated sugar to garnish

Method:

1. Put the eggs, caster sugar, Grand Marnier, cream and vanilla into a large bowl and whisk to combine.
2. Slice the bread at an angle into 2 inch-thick slices. Place the slices into an oblong baking dish such as a lasagne dish. Pour the egg mixture over the bread. Allow it to soak up some of egg mixture, and then carefully turn the bread over. *At this point the mixture can be prepared, covered, and refrigerated overnight. Allow the bread to absorb all of the egg mixture – this will take about 1 hour.*
3. Melt the butter in a large non-stick skillet over a medium heat. Add the oil, place the bread in a pan and cook until it's golden brown, then turn it over and repeat the process. The bread will puff up while cooking. If you doubt that bread is cooked all the way through, place into a preheated oven for 5 to 10 minutes.
4. Dust with granulated sugar and serve on warmed plates.

Syrup is not necessary, but can be used if desired.

Gingerbread Crepes with Sautéed Apples

Makes 12 crepes

Crepes

140g / 5oz strong white flour
2 tbsps caster sugar
1 tsp ground ginger
1 tsp ground cinnamon
Pinch of cloves
Pinch of allspice
275ml / 11 fluid oz milk
2 eggs
50ml / 2 fluid oz black treacle or molasses
1 tbsp butter, melted

Crepes method:

1. Combine all of the dry ingredients in a food processor. Combine the milk, eggs, treacle and butter in a jug; pour this mixture into the dry ingredients through a feed tube. Whisk to combine, but do not over-mix. Can also be done with electric mixer.
2. Heat the crepe pan, and then lightly butter it. Pour 55g / 2oz batter onto the pan, tilt pan to evenly distribute batter and cook until the crepe looks solid – about 2 minutes. Flip the crepe over and cook it for about 1 minute more. Turn it out onto parchment paper, and keep warm until they're all ready to serve. Place layers of parchment between crepes to prevent sticking together.

Apples:

2 tbsps butter
4 Granny Smith apples, peeled, cored, cut into eighths
100ml / 4 fluid oz hot water

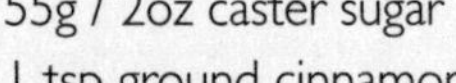

55g / 2oz caster sugar
1 tsp ground cinnamon
1 tsp lemon juice
1 tbsp brandy
2 tbsps raisins
55g / 2oz toasted hazelnuts, chopped
Whipped cream to garnish

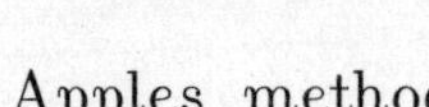

Apples method:

Melt the butter in a deep-sided frying pan. Add the apples, and then toss them in the pan to coat them in butter. Add the sugar, cinnamon, raisins, brandy and lemon juice. Sauté for a few minutes; when the mixture begins to boil add hot water and cook uncovered for 10 minutes. Cook just until the apples are tender when pierced with a skewer. Do not let them get mushy. The sauce should be syrupy – if it is runny take the apples out and boil to reduce the sauce to syrup.

Serving:

Place one crepe on a warmed plate, and then spoon the apples down the centre of the crepe. Fold both sides of the crepe over apples. Drizzle with syrup, then sprinkle with toasted hazelnuts and garnish with a dollop of whipped cream.

To easily measure treacle or molasses, simply coat measuring cup with a drop of oil. Treacle or molasses will slip out of cup, making measuring and clean-up a snap.

Sausage Breakfast Bread Pudding

Serves 8
Preheat oven to 180C (350F)

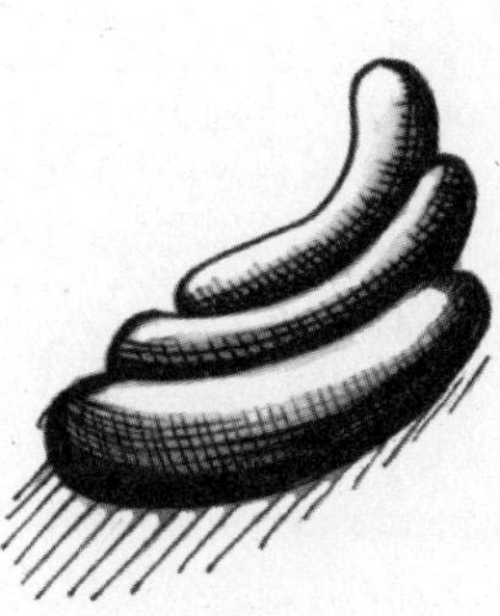

455g / 16oz bulk sausage meat
6 eggs
400ml / 16 fluid oz milk
1 tsp dry mustard
1 Granny Smith apple, peeled, cored, and diced fine
1 tsp rubbed sage
6 slices white bread, crust removed and cut into 1-inch pieces
4–6 mushrooms, diced
170g / 6oz grated cheddar cheese

Method:

1. Cook the sausage meat in a frying pan, and use a wooden spoon to break the sausage into smallish pieces. Drain the pieces on a paper towel and set aside.
2. Whisk the eggs in a large bowl. Add the milk, mustard and sage. Whisk to combine.
3. Butter a 9x13-inch baking dish. Cover the bottom with bread cubes. Sprinkle the sausage meat over the bread, then the apple, mushrooms and finally the grated cheddar cheese. Pour the egg mixture over the contents of the baking dish. Cover the mixture with cling film and refrigerate overnight.
4. Remove the mixture from the refrigerator and bring it to room temperature. Bake uncovered at 180C (350F) for 40–50 minutes or until the centre tests done, when a knife inserted into the centre comes out clean. Garnish with a grilled tomato.

Sautéed Lamb Kidneys with Mustard Sauce on Toast

Serves 4

680g / 24oz lamb kidneys
40g / 1½oz butter
½ tsp minced garlic
1 tsp minced shallot
1 tsp Dalkey (or whole seed) mustard
2 tsps lemon juice
3 tbsps brandy
50ml / 2 fluid oz chicken stock
75ml / 3 fluid oz cream

Method:

1. Halve each kidney lengthwise through the core. With a kitchen scissors cut out the white core.
2. Heat the butter in a frying pan, then sauté the kidneys for 2 minutes on each side or until they are golden brown and just firm. (The kidneys should be pink in the centre and juicy.) Remove from the pan and keep warm.
3. Sauté the garlic and shallot in the frying pan, scraping up any bits. Add the mustard, lemon juice, brandy and chicken stock. Bring to the boil and reduce by half. Add cream and cook until it has thickened.
4. Toast the bread, and place on a warmed plate. Top with a serving of kidneys. Spoon the sauce over the kidneys.

Garnish with a sprinkle of chopped fresh parsley.

Smoked Salmon with Scrambled Eggs

Serves 1

2–3 slices Irish smoked salmon
2 eggs
Splash of cream
Butter

Method:

1. Line a 140g / 5oz ramekin with slices of smoked salmon, with edges of fish overhanging the edge of the ramekin.
2. Place the eggs in a bowl, and add a splash of cream and whisk together.
3. Warm a saucepan. Melt in the butter and add the eggs. Stir until the desired texture is obtained.
4. Spoon the scrambled egg into the ramekin and fold over the overhanging salmon to cover. Turn out onto the toasted bread and garnish with lengths of chives and lemon crème fraiche.

Lemon Crème Fraiche

200ml / 8 fluid oz crème fraiche
2 tsps finely grated lemon zest

Method:

Combine zest and crème fraiche. Chill for 30 minutes to allow the flavours to marry.

Sweet Onion & Thyme Leaf Tart

Serves 6
Preheat oven to 180C (350F)

100ml / 4 fluid oz milk
100ml / 4 fluid oz cream
1 tbsp sunflower oil
1 tbsp butter
3 eggs, beaten
115g / 4oz grated Emmental cheese
¼ tsp thyme leaves, fresh
¼ tsp black pepper
Pinch of nutmeg
1 9-inch shortcrust tart shell

Shortcrust

365g / 13oz strong white flour
1 tsp salt
1 tsp caster sugar
225g / 8oz butter
50ml / 2 fluid oz ice water

Shortcrust method:

1. Combine the flour, salt, and sugar in a large bowl.
2. Cut the butter into 1-inch cubes. With a pastry blender or knife cut the butter into the flour until the mixture resembles coarse crumbs. This can also be done with a food processor. Add water and work the mixture into a ball. If the pastry does not come together, add more water a few drops at a time. Divide the dough in half. Flatten the dough into 2 discs and wrap it in cling film. Chill for 30 minutes. (Freeze one for later use.)

3. Remove the dough from the refrigerator and bring to room temperature. Roll it out between 2 sheets of cling film and fill a tart pan (with removable bottom). Chill the dough again for another 30 minutes before baking – this helps prevent shrinkage.

Filling method:

1. Melt the butter in a sauté pan or a skillet over medium heat. Add the oil and sauté the onions until they are soft. Set them aside to cool.
2. Combine the onions, milk, eggs, cheese, herbs and seasonings. Pour them into a prepared tart crust and bake for 30 minutes or until a knife inserted into the centre comes out clean.

Serve with apple wedges and Hashbrowns Supreme (see page 39).

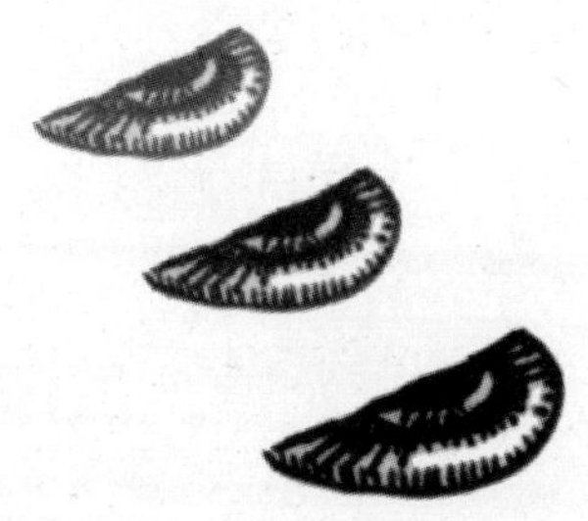

Soups

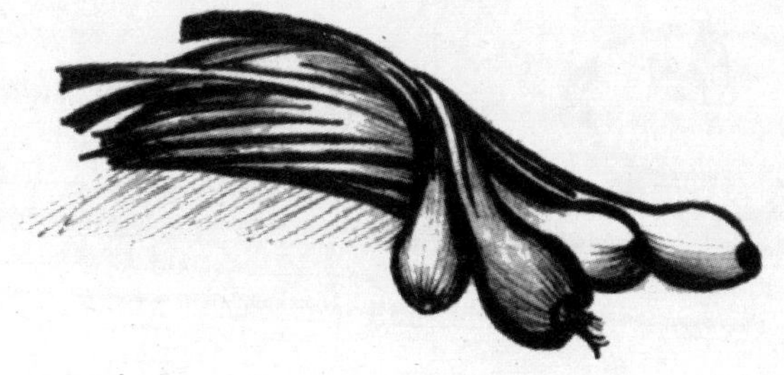

Beef Stock

Makes about 2 litres / 64 fluid oz depending on reduction during cooking.
Preheat oven to 200C (400F)

1800g / 64oz beef bones
– shank works well
455g / 16oz oxtail or rib bones
2 medium yellow onions, quartered
2 leeks, white and pale green part only, cut into four pieces
2 stalks celery, use leaves, cut into four pieces
2 medium carrots, cut into 4 pieces
2 shallots, quartered
2 bay leaves
2 sprigs parsley
8 black peppercorns
4 whole cloves
2 litres / 64 fluid oz cold water

Method:

1. Ask your butcher to cut bones into 4-inch pieces. Place the bones in a roasting pan and roast them for 1 hour at 200C (400F).
2. Place the roasted bones and the remainder of the ingredients into a large stockpot, cover with a lid and bring to boil. Reduce the heat and simmer for 6 hours, adding more water if needed.
3. Strain into a large pot or bowl, chill, and skim off the fat. Pour into sterile freezer containers and freeze until needed.

Plastic milk or cream bottles in a variety of sizes work great as containers.

Chicken Stock

Makes about 2 litres / 64 fluid oz depending on reduction during cooking.

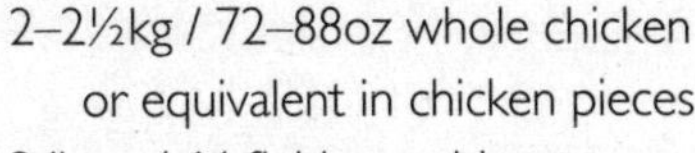

2–2½kg / 72–88oz whole chicken or equivalent in chicken pieces
2 litres / 64 fluid oz cold water
2 shallots, cut into quarters
2 medium yellow onions, cut into four pieces
2 stalks celery, use leaves, cut into four pieces
2 medium carrots, cut into four pieces
2 leeks, white and pale green part only, cut into four pieces
2 sprigs parsley
8 black peppercorns
1 sprig thyme
1 bay leaf

Method:

1. Coarsely chop the chicken. Place into a large stockpot. Add the remaining ingredients and bring to boil. Cover with a lid, reduce heat and allow to simmer for 6–8 hours.
2. Strain into a large pot or bowl and allow to cool completely. Chill and skim off the fat. Pour into sterile freezer containers and freeze until needed.

Fish Stock

Makes about 2 litres / 64 fluid oz
depending on reduction during cooking.

1350–1800g / 48–64oz fish bones
250ml / 8 fluid oz dry white wine
2 bay leaves
2 parsley sprigs
2 thyme sprigs
2 litres / 64 fluid oz cold water

Method:

1. Place all of the ingredients in a large stockpot. Cover and bring to boil. Reduce the heat and simmer for 1–2 hours.
2. Strain, cool, and freeze in sterile freezer containers until needed. Plastic milk or cream bottles work well.

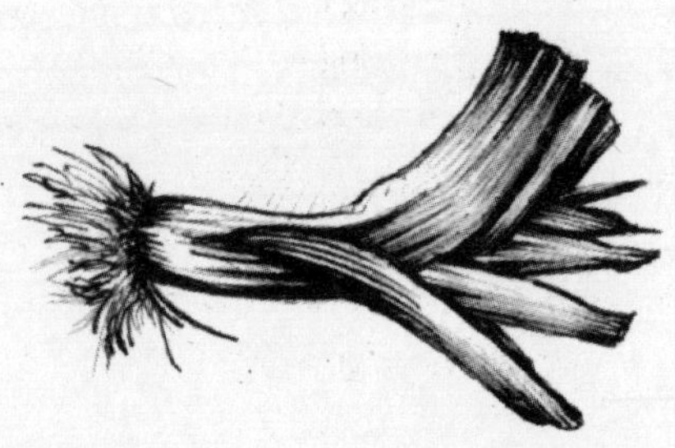

Lamb Stock

Makes about 2 litres / 64 fluid oz
depending on the amount of reduction during cooking.
Preheat oven to 200C (400F)

1800g / 64oz lamb or mutton with bones, cut into pieces
2 litres / 64 fluid oz cold water
2 medium yellow onions, quartered
2 shallots, quartered
2 leeks, white and pale green parts only, cut into four pieces
2 stalks celery, use leaves, cut into four pieces
3 sprigs parsley
8 black peppercorns
4 whole cloves
3 bay leaves
2 sprigs thyme

Method:

1. Roast the lamb in roasting pan at 200C (400F) for 1 hour.
2. Place the lamb and remaining ingredients into a large stock-pot. Cover with a lid and bring to the boil. Reduce the heat and simmer for 8 hours. Check the pot occasionally, adding more water if needed.
3. Strain into a large pot and boil to reduce by half. Chill, skim the fat off and pour into sterile freezer containers (plastic milk or cream bottles work great!).

Freeze until needed.

Basic Vegetable Soup

Serves 8

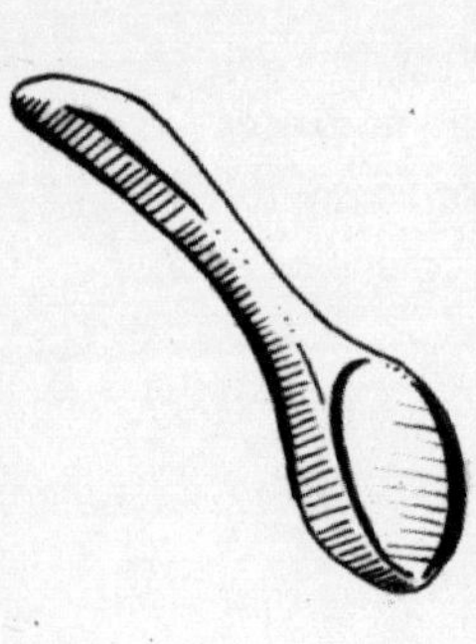

55g / 2oz butter
140g / 5oz potato, peeled and diced
115g / 4oz onion, diced
1 clove garlic, minced
340g / 12oz vegetables of choice, chopped
1 litre / 32 fluid oz chicken stock
100ml / 4 fluid oz equal parts milk and cream
100ml / 4 fluid oz dry white wine
Salt and pepper

Method:

1. Melt the butter in a heavy-bottomed pan, add the onions and garlic and sauté until fragrant. Add the potatoes and your vegetables of choice and toss to coat. Cover with a parchment lid, then with an oven lid. Reduce the heat and sweat the vegetables for 10 minutes or until tender. Check periodically to ensure the vegetables do not brown.
2. Add the stock and wine and simmer for approximately 20 minutes or until vegetables are soft.
3. Puree in a blender, add the creamy milk, and adjust the seasoning.

Serve in a warmed bowl garnished with cream, crème fraiche, herbs or cheese.

Apple & Cheddar Soup

Serves 6–8

55g / 2oz butter
115g / 4oz onion, chopped
1 leek, white part only, chopped
1 Granny Smith apple,
peeled, cored, diced
140g / 5oz potato, peeled, cut into dice
1 litre / 32 fluid oz chicken stock
225g / 8oz grated sharp
cheddar cheese
100ml / 4 fluid oz equal parts
milk and cream
¼ tsp dried thyme
Salt and pepper to taste

Method:

1. Melt the butter in a heavy-bottomed pan, then add the onion, leeks and apple. Sauté for a few minutes or until the mixture becomes fragrant. Add the potato and toss in the mixture to coat. Cover with a parchment lid, then with a saucepan lid. Lower the heat and allow the vegetables to sweat for approximately 10 minutes. Check to ensure the vegetables do not brown.
2. Add the stock and thyme, then simmer for 20 minutes.
3. Puree the soup in a blender. Add the cheese and stir to melt it into the soup. Add creamy milk and re-heat if needed.
4. Garnish with crispy fried streaky bacon and a pinch of finely grated cheddar cheese.

A slice of warm brown bread on the side makes this a great meal.

Asparagus Soup with Lemongrass

Serves 8

55g / 2oz butter
140g / 5oz potato, peeled and diced
115g / 4oz onion, diced
340g / 12oz asparagus, chopped
1 litre / 32 fluid oz chicken stock
2 two-inch pieces of lemongrass
100ml / 4 fluid oz equal parts cream and milk
6 fresh basil leaves
Sprig of parsley
Salt and pepper

Method:

1. Melt the butter in a heavy-bottomed pan. Add the potato and onion and stir to coat them in butter. Sauté for a couple of minutes. Cover with a parchment lid, then with a saucepan lid and let the mix sweat until tender. This should take approximately 10 minutes. Add the herbs, then bruise the lemongrass with the flat side of a knife and add to the pan. Add the stock and simmer for 20 minutes. Add the asparagus, and simmer uncovered (the asparagus will retain a lovely green colour if uncovered) for 10 minutes.
2. Remove the lemongrass. Puree the soup in a blender until smooth; add the creamy milk and season to taste. Warm gently and serve. Garnish with a drizzle of cream and some julienned basil leaves.

To julienne the basil leaves, gently roll leaves into a tube shape and slice thinly with a very sharp knife or kitchen shears. Do this just before serving to prevent discoloration of the basil.

Butternut Squash Soup with Apple & Fresh Thyme

Serves 8

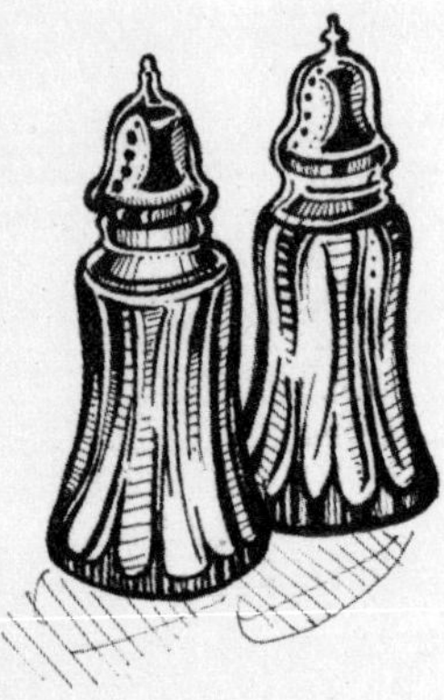

55g / 2oz butter
455g / 16oz butternut squash, diced
1 Granny Smith apple, peeled, cored and diced
115g / 4oz onion, diced
1 clove garlic, minced
600ml / 24 fluid oz chicken stock
2 tsps fresh thyme leaves
100ml / 4 fluid oz equal parts milk and cream
¼ tsp cumin
Salt and pepper to taste

Method:

1. Melt the butter in a heavy-bottomed pan. Add the onion and garlic and sauté until fragrant. Add the squash and apple and stir to coat them in the butter. Cover with a parchment lid, then with a saucepan lid. Reduce the heat and allow to sweat for 10 minutes. Check periodically to ensure the vegetables are not browning.
2. Add the stock, thyme, and cumin. Simmer for 20 minutes or until the vegetables are tender.
3. Puree in a blender, add creamy milk, and serve.

Garnish with crème fraiche.

Celeriac Soup with Cashel Blue Croutons

Serves 8

55g / 2oz butter
1 large celeriac, peeled, cut into dice
140g / 5oz potato, peeled and diced
115g / 4oz onion, diced
1 clove garlic, minced
½ tsp dried thyme leaves
½ tsp dried parsley
1 litre / 32 fluid oz chicken stock
100ml / 4 fluid oz dry white wine
100ml / 4 fluid oz equal parts cream and milk
Pinch of salt and pepper

Method:

1. Melt the butter in a heavy-bottomed pan. Add the onion, herbs and garlic. Sauté until fragrant, then add the potato and celeriac. Cover with a parchment lid, then with a saucepan lid. Reduce the heat and leave to sweat for 10 minutes. Check periodically to ensure the vegetables do not brown.
2. Add the wine, then stir and allow it to reduce a bit. Add the stock and simmer until the vegetables are soft.
3. Puree the mix in a blender, add the creamy milk, and season to taste.

Dice Cashel Blue into ¼-inch squares and drop into the soup to garnish.

Dublin Bay Prawn Bisque

Serves 8
Preheat oven to 200C (400F)

340g / 12oz butter
455g / 16oz Dublin Bay prawns, meat and shells
2 carrots, diced

1 onion, diced
2 leeks, white part only, chopped
3 stalks celery, chopped
2 bay leaves
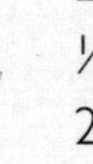
½ tsp black peppercorns
2 tsps tomato paste
85g / 3oz flour
150ml / 6 fluid oz dry white wine
200ml / 8 fluid oz cream

2 tsps brandy
200ml / 8 fluid oz tomato juice
½ tsp cayenne

Method:

1. Remove the prawn meat from the shell and set aside. In a heavy roasting pan sauté the prawn shells in ½ of the butter for 10 minutes. Add the rest of the vegetables and roast in an oven for 1 hour.
2. Melt the remaining butter in a heavy-bottomed pan; add the shells, vegetables, bay leaves, peppercorns and tomato paste. Sauté for 10 minutes, add the flour and stir to blend. Add wine and enough water to cover. Simmer covered for 1 hour.
3. Remove the shells. Puree the vegetables and stock in a blender. Strain to remove any bits and add the cream. Add

the brandy, cayenne and salt (if needed), and then warm gently. Chop the prawn meat and add to the soup. Cook for 2 minutes – just enough to cook the prawns.

4. Dilute the soup to desired consistency by adding tomato juice.

Drizzle with some cream and serve.

Autumn Mushroom Soup

Serves 8

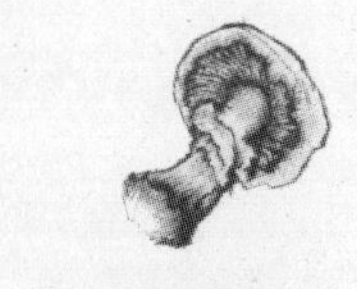

6–8 large field mushrooms
4 dried shitake mushrooms
1 small onion, diced
2 small potatoes, peeled and diced
½ tsp dried thyme
½ tsp dried basil
¼ tsp celery salt
400ml / 16 fluid oz chicken stock
1 tsp soy sauce
3 tbsps brandy
3 tbsps cream sherry
3 tbsps butter
100ml / 4 fluid oz cream
Salt and pepper to taste

Method:

1. Melt the butter in a heavy-bottomed pan and add the diced onion and potato. Cover with a parchment lid, and then with a saucepan lid and allow to sweat for 10 minutes. Check to ensure the vegetables do not brown.
2. Re-hydrate the shitake mushrooms with 100ml / 4 fluid oz boiling water for 30 minutes. Drain, rinse well, then slice off and discard the stems. Brush and wipe clean the field mushrooms and then slice. Add the mushrooms, herbs, stock, soy sauce, sherry and brandy to the pan. Bring to the boil, reduce heat and simmer covered for 20 minutes.
3. Puree in a blender. Add cream, taste and adjust seasoning. Re-heat if needed.

Serve in warmed bowls.

Leek & Pear Soup

Serves 8

55g / 2oz butter
4 leeks, white part only, sliced
2 Bosc pears, peeled and cut into dice
2 potatoes, peeled and diced
1 litre / 32 fluid oz chicken stock
2 tsps dried tarragon
2 tsps parsley, fresh
100ml / 4 fluid oz dry white wine
1 tsp soy sauce
100ml / 4 fluid oz equal parts
cream and milk
Salt and pepper to taste

Method:

1. Melt the butter in a heavy-bottomed pan, add the leeks and sauté until soft.
2. Add the potatoes and pears then cover with a parchment lid and then with a saucepan lid. Reduce the heat and sweat for 10 minutes. Do not allow the vegetables to brown.
3. Add the herbs, wine, soy sauce, and stock. Simmer for 20 minutes.
4. Puree in a blender, add the creamy milk, and adjust the seasoning if necessary.

Serve in warmed bowls with a swirl of cream and some parsley.

Lentil Soup

Serves 8

455g / 16oz brown lentils
1200ml / 40 fluid oz chicken stock
340g / 2oz canned plum tomatoes, diced
100ml / 4 fluid oz dry white wine
3 large carrots, diced
1 large onion, diced
2 stalks celery, diced
3 cloves garlic, minced
½ tsp dried basil
½ tsp dried marjoram
¼ tsp dried thyme
1 bay leaf
2 tbsps dried parsley
1 tsp salt
Pinch of nutmeg
2 tbsps apple cider vinegar

Method:

1. Combine the stock, 600ml / 20 fluid oz water, wine, and canned tomatoes in a large soup pot.
2. Add the washed lentils, vegetables, and herbs. Bring to the boil, reduce heat and simmer for 45 to 60 minutes, or until the lentils are tender.
3. Stir in the vinegar and serve.

Garnish with a swirl of sour cream. This is a meal in a bowl, serve with Cheddar Pepper Bread (see page 148) to warm a chilly evening.

Minestrone Soup

Serves 8

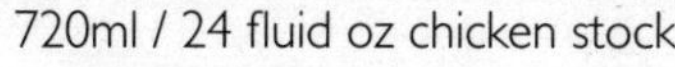

720ml / 24 fluid oz chicken stock
2 medium onions, diced
2 large carrots, diced
1 stalk celery, diced
2 medium potatoes, peeled and diced
1 courgette, diced
115g / 4oz French green beans, cut into ½-inch pieces
225g / 8oz can red kidney beans, drained and rinsed
2 plum tomatoes, peeled, seeded and diced
225g / 8oz spinach, roughly chopped
2 cloves garlic, minced
2 tbsps olive oil

Method:

1. Heat the oil in a heavy-bottomed pan. Sauté the garlic, onions, carrots, celery, and potatoes for a couple of minutes. Cover with a parchment lid, and then with a saucepan lid. Allow the mix to sweat for 10 minutes.
2. Add the stock and tomatoes and bring to the boil. Reduce the heat and simmer for 10 to 20 minutes, until the vegetables are just tender. Add the green beans, courgette, kidney beans, and spinach. Cook uncovered for 10 minutes.
3. Season with some salt and pepper.

Garnish with freshly grated Parmesan cheese.

Roasted Pumpkin Soup

Serves 8
Preheat oven to 225C (425F)

900g / 32oz roasted pumpkin pulp
3 cloves garlic, minced
2 tbsps olive oil
1 medium onion, diced
1 tbsp fresh ginger, minced
200ml / 8 fluid oz dry white wine
1 litre / 32 fluid oz chicken stock
1 tsp sweet chilli sauce
1 tsp cumin
Soy sauce to taste
Crème fraiche to garnish

Method:

1. Place the seeded pumpkin on a baking sheet. Drizzle with 1 tbsp of olive oil. Roast until it is tender when pierced with a skewer – about 40 minutes. Cool, peel, and puree in a blender. The pumpkin can be prepared to this point and frozen for later use.
2. Heat 1 tbsp of oil in a heavy-bottomed pan. Add the onion, garlic and ginger. Sauté until fragrant, then add the wine and reduce by half. Add the pumpkin and stock, and simmer for 30 minutes.
3. Add the chilli sauce and cumin. Puree the soup in a blender, and season with soy sauce.
4. Ladle into warmed bowls, garnish with some crème fraiche.

Serve additional chilli sauce for those with a spicier palate.

Rustic Tomato Soup

Serves 8

680g / 24oz passata
400g / 14oz canned chopped plum tomatoes
115g / 4oz onion, chopped
1 clove garlic, minced
1 tsp fresh basil, chopped
55g / 2oz butter
½ tsp sugar
½ tsp salt
½ tsp pepper
25ml / 1 fluid oz gin
200ml / 8 fluid oz chicken stock
100ml / 4 fluid oz cream
Streaky rasher lardons cooked crisp

Method:

1. Heat the butter in a large soup pot. Add the onion and garlic, and sauté until soft. Add the passata, chopped plum tomatoes, herbs, sugar, salt and pepper. Stir in the stock and gin. Simmer for 20 minutes.
2. Puree in a blender to achieve the desired consistency – some lumps can be nice for a rustic effect.

Serve in warmed bowls with crispy bacon bits.

Spiced Onion Soup

Serves 8

Spice mixture

1 tsp cayenne pepper
1 tsp dried thyme
1 tsp dried oregano
1 tsp dried basil
½ tsp white pepper
6 bay leaves

Combine and set aside.

Soup

100ml / 4 fluid oz sunflower oil
115g / 4oz flour
1350g / 48oz thinly sliced mild onions
1½ tsps salt
2 tbsps minced garlic
1½ litres / 48 fluid oz chicken stock
100ml / 4 fluid oz dry white wine
115g / 4oz grated white cheddar
115g / 4oz grated yellow cheddar
55g / 2oz grated Emmental cheese
55g / 2oz grated Parmesan cheese

Method:

1. In a heavy-bottomed pan combine the oil and flour. Over a medium heat stir for 10 minutes to make a soft brown roux.
2. Add the onions and half of the spice mixture. Stir to combine and cook for 8 minutes or until the onions are soft and golden. Add the garlic and sauté for an additional 2 minutes.

3. Add the stock and wine. Stir to loosen any brown bits. Reduce the heat to low and simmer for 45 minutes. Remove the bay leaves.
4. Combine the cheddars and Emmental, then slowly add to the soup, stirring until the cheese melts.
5. Taste for seasoning; add more of spice mix if desired.

Serve in heated bowls with a sprinkle of Parmesan cheese.

Salads

Wild Rice Salad

Serves 6–8

310g / 11oz wild rice
600ml / 24 fluid oz cold water
¼ tsp salt
1 Granny Smith apple, peeled, cored, and cut into dice
115g / 4oz red bell pepper
115g / 4oz raisins
115g / 4oz pecans, toasted and chopped
55g / 2oz diced red onion
55g / 2oz dried apricots, diced
55g/ 2oz dried cranberries
1 tbsp balsamic vinegar
1 tbsp red wine vinegar
2 tbsps olive oil
Salt and pepper to taste

Method:

1. Rinse the rice well, place into a saucepan and add water and salt. Bring to the boil, reduce the heat, cover and simmer for 20–30 minutes. The rice should be just tender, not soft or mushy. Texture is the key. Drain the rice and place into a large bowl.
2. Add the apple, red pepper, onion, pecans and dried fruits to the wild rice.
3. Combine the vinegars and oil, whisking all the time. Season with salt and pepper. Pour over the salad and stir to combine. Chill for 1 hour and serve.

This salad is best served on the day it is made.

Creamy Parmesan with Cracked Black Pepper Dressing

Serves 8

1 small clove garlic, crushed
1 large fresh egg yolk
1 tsp Dijon mustard
2 tbsps lemon juice
4 tbsps finely grated Parmesan cheese
100ml / 4 fluid oz olive oil
40ml / 1½ fluid oz sunflower oil
2 tbsps cream
½ tsp coarsely cracked black pepper

Method:

1. Put the garlic, egg yolk, mustard, lemon juice, and Parmesan into a small bowl. Whisk together with a mixer or in a food processor, just to blend.
2. Very slowly whisk in the oils to make a smooth dressing.
3. Stir in the cream and pepper.

Add salt to taste and refrigerate until needed.

Dried Herb Dressing

Makes about 4 servings

400ml / 16 fluid oz sunflower oil
200ml / 8 fluid oz olive oil
200ml / 8 fluid oz red wine vinegar
1 egg
50ml / 2 fluid oz honey
2 tbsps dried tarragon
1 tbsp dried marjoram
2 tsps dried basil
1 tsp dried thyme
1 clove garlic, minced
1 tsp black pepper
¼ tsp sea salt

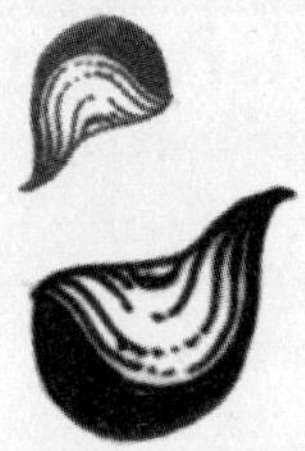

Method:

1. Place the vinegar, herbs garlic, pepper, salt, and egg in a food processor.
2. Add the oils in a slow, steady stream, speeding up as the dressing thickens.

Store in a covered jar in the refrigerator. This dressing will keep for at least a week.

Fresh Herb Vinaigrette

Makes about 200ml / 8 fluid oz

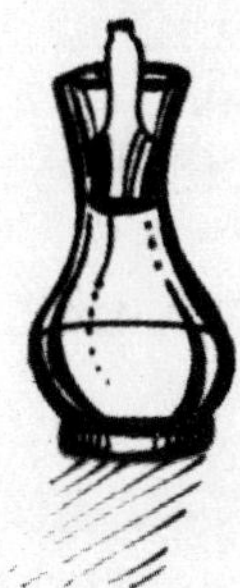

100ml / 4 fluid oz sunflower oil
50ml / 2 fluid oz olive oil
2 tbsps cider vinegar
2 tsps honey
Small handful of fresh lemon thyme
leaves, parsley, mint, and basil
Salt and pepper to taste

Method:

1. Put all of the ingredients in a blender and process to a smooth dressing. Chill until needed.

This dressing will keep for a few days in the refrigerator.

Honey Mustard Vinaigrette

Makes about 350ml / 14 fluid oz

25ml / 1 fluid oz honey
55g / 2 oz Dijon mustard
40ml / 1½ fluid oz white balsamic vinegar
50ml / 2 fluid oz sunflower oil
150ml / 6 fluid oz olive oil
Dash of Tabasco sauce
1 tsp Dalkey mustard (or other coarse seed mustard)
¼ tsp salt

Method:

1. Combine the honey, Dijon, balsamic, Dalkey mustard, Tabasco and salt in a small mixing bowl.
2. Combine the oils in a measuring jug and slowly add to the bowl while whisking.

Serve over spinach, coz lettuce, or greens of choice.

Papaya Seed Dressing

Makes about 1 litre / 32 fluid oz

225g / 8oz caster sugar
1 tsp salt
1 tsp dry mustard
200ml / 8 fluid oz white wine vinegar
400ml / 16 fluid oz sunflower oil
1 shallot, minced
3 tbsps fresh papaya seeds
1 tsp freshly squeezed lime juice

Method:

1. Place the sugar, salt, and mustard into a blender jar. Add the vinegar, lime juice and shallot and blitz to blend.
2. With motor running, gradually add the oil. Add the seeds and blend until seeds are the size of coarse ground black pepper.

Serve on greens or fresh fruit.

Red Salad Dressing

Makes about 200ml / 8 fluid oz

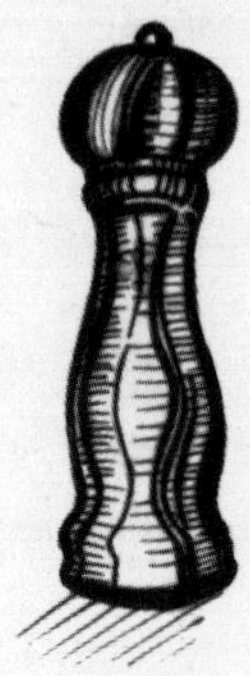

100ml / 4 fluid oz ketchup
1 tbsp salt
1 tsp sugar
1 tbsp dry mustard
2 tsps sweet paprika
½ tsp cayenne
4 tbsps Worcestershire sauce
400ml / 16 fluid oz red wine vinegar
600ml / 25 fluid oz sunflower oil

Method:

1. Combine all of the ingredients in a blender and blitz.
2. Pour into a covered jar and refrigerate. Will keep for a couple of weeks in refrigerator.

Serve with greens, red onion and tomato wedges.

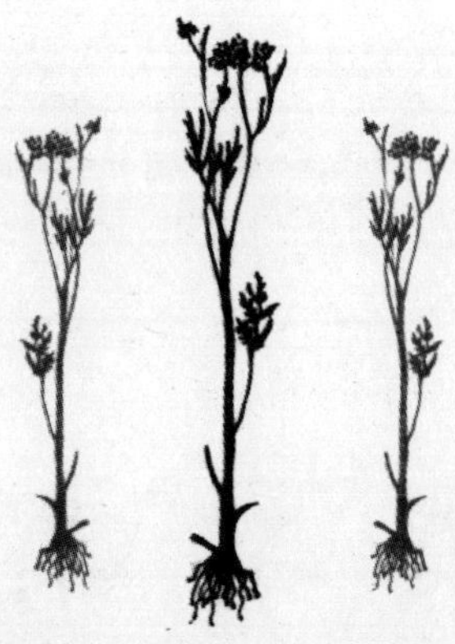

Farro Salad

Serves 4 to 6

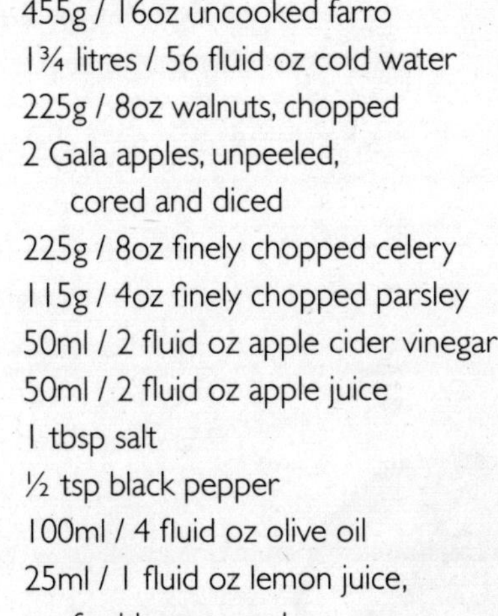

455g / 16oz uncooked farro
1¾ litres / 56 fluid oz cold water
225g / 8oz walnuts, chopped
2 Gala apples, unpeeled, cored and diced
225g / 8oz finely chopped celery
115g / 4oz finely chopped parsley
50ml / 2 fluid oz apple cider vinegar
50ml / 2 fluid oz apple juice
1 tbsp salt
½ tsp black pepper
100ml / 4 fluid oz olive oil
25ml / 1 fluid oz lemon juice, freshly squeezed

Method:

1. Soak the farro overnight in water to cover by 3 inches.
2. In a saucepan, bring the water to boil, add the drained farro and simmer uncovered for 40 to 60 minutes, or until thoroughly cooked. The texture should be firm and somewhat chewy, not mushy. Drain and set aside to cool.
3. Prepare the dressing by combining the cider vinegar, apple juice, lemon juice, salt and pepper, and slowly whisking in the oil.
4. In a large bowl, mix the farro, walnuts, apple, celery and parsley, and toss with the dressing.

Chill and serve.

Picnic Pasta Salad

Serves 4

200g / 7oz pasta spirals
4 eggs, hardboiled
225g / 8oz French green beans, cut into ½-inch lengths
225g / 8oz broccoli, separated into bite-size florets
6–8 cherry tomatoes
115g / 4oz red bell pepper
115g / 4oz pitted black olives
225g / 8oz sliced scallion
225g / 8oz matchstick cut courgette
1 can flaked tuna steak, in water

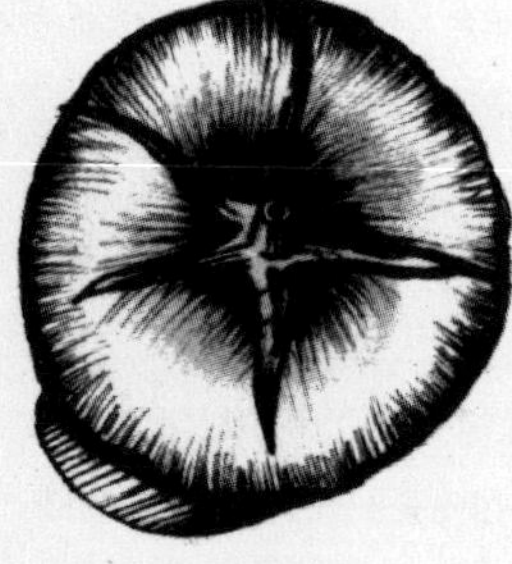

Combine:

½ tsp dried oregano
½ tsp dried dill weed
¼ tsp dried basil
¼ tsp dried tarragon
1 tsp dried parsley

Dressing

1 tsp salt
300ml / 12 fluid oz olive oil
100ml / 4 fluid oz mayonnaise (preferably homemade)
½ tsp black pepper
75ml / 3 fluid oz red wine vinegar
1 tsp balsamic vinegar

Method:

1. Cook the pasta as directed on the package. Drain and rinse well. Set aside in a large bowl.
2. In a large saucepan bring water to the boil; blanch the green beans until they are crisp but tender. Remove the beans with a slotted spoon and plunge into some ice water. Repeat this process for the broccoli. Very briefly dip the red pepper and courgette into the boiling water and then dip them in the ice water, after no longer than ½ minute. The purpose is to take away the rawness of the vegetables but not to cook them.
3. Drain all of the vegetables and add to the pasta.
4. Toss the herb combination into the pasta / vegetable mixture.
5. Mix the dressing ingredients in a bowl and whisk to combine. Toss the salad with the dressing. Garnish with quartered boiled eggs, flaked tuna and halved cherry tomatoes. Cover, chill, and serve.

Best served on the day it is made.

Spinach Salad with Cranberry Dressing

Serves 4–6

115g / 4oz fresh or frozen cranberries
55g / 2oz caster sugar
100ml / 4 fluid oz white wine vinegar
¼ tsp Tabasco sauce
1 tsp Dijon mustard
100ml / 4 fluid oz sunflower oil
50ml / 2 fluid oz olive oil
Salt and pepper to taste
225g / 8oz baby spinach leaves
1 small red onion, sliced in thin rings
6–8 mushrooms, sliced
115g / 4oz julienned cooked beets
55g / 2oz toasted chopped hazelnuts
85–115g / 3–4oz crumbled feta cheese
170g / 6oz streaky bacon, ¼ inch dice, cooked crisp

Method:

1. Prepare the cranberry dressing; combine the cranberries, sugar and vinegar in a saucepan, cook over a medium heat until the cranberries pop (for about 5 minutes). Remove from the heat, cool and puree in a blender.
2. Add the Tabasco, Dijon, oils, salt and pepper to the blender. Chill the mixture until it is ready to use.
3. Combine the spinach, red onion, mushrooms, beets and streaky bacon in a large salad bowl. Toss with the dressing. Garnish with some feta cheese and hazelnuts.

Toss the salad in the dressing just before serving to prevent it from wilting.

Sides & Vegetables

Asian Green Beans

Serves 4–6

455g / 16oz fresh green beans
2 scallions, sliced finely at an angle
2 cloves garlic, minced
2 tsps fresh ginger, minced
2 tbsps sesame oil
1 tbsp oyster sauce
¼ tsp chilli flakes
55g / 2oz flaked almonds, toasted
1 tsp white sesame seeds, toasted

Method:

1. Blanch the green beans in boiling water for 2–4 minutes or until they are crisp but tender. Drain and plunge the beans into ice water to stop the cooking process. Set them aside until needed. This can be done in advance.
2. Heat the sesame oil in a sauté pan. Add the garlic and ginger, then sauté until fragrant (½ to 1 minute). Add the scallions and stir to combine. Add the drained green beans, oyster sauce and chilli flakes. Stir to coat the beans and then warm to serving temperature.

Place into a warmed dish and garnish with almonds and sesame seeds.

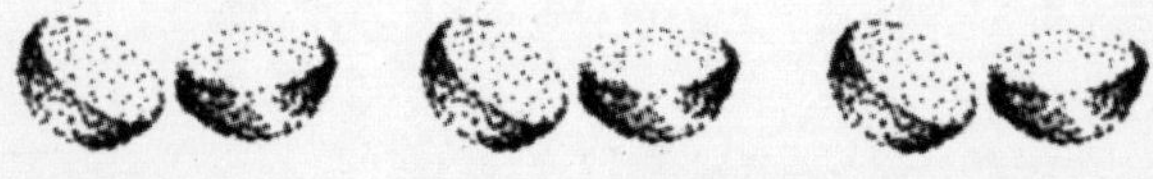

Beet Tartar

455g / 16oz cooked beets, minced
1 shallot, minced
2 tbsps capers, chopped
8 cornichons, minced
1 tsp Worcestershire sauce
1 tsp Tabasco sauce
1 tsp raspberry vinegar
1 tbsp olive oil
2 tbsps chopped fresh chives
1 tbsp minced fresh dill
Salt and pepper to taste

Method:

1. Combine all of the ingredients in a bowl. Stir to blend, cover and chill.

Serve as a salad or as a garnish.

Braised Peas

Serves 4–6

3 tbsps butter
6 shallots, sliced
1 clove garlic, minced
455g / 16oz frozen petit peas
175ml / 7 fluid oz chicken stock
1–2 tsps grated lemon zest

Method:

1. Melt 2 tbsps butter in a saucepan. Add the shallots and garlic, and cook until they are soft and translucent.
2. Add the chicken stock, bring to the boil, and add the peas. Reduce heat and simmer for 5 minutes.
3. Strain, reserve the liquid, and keep the peas warm. Boil the liquid to reduce it to a glaze, then toss in the peas to coat. Warm gently and add 1 tbsp butter.

Garnish with some grated lemon zest.

Cashel Blue Potato Bake

Serves 6

1.5kg / 48oz rooster potatoes
2 tbsps sunflower oil
1 tbsp butter
2 medium onions, chopped
2 cloves garlic, minced
2 tsps fresh rosemary, chopped
2 tsps fresh parsley, chopped
¼ tsp fresh thyme, chopped
¼ tsp dried mustard
115g / 4oz butter
150ml / 6 fluid oz cream
25ml / 1 fluid oz brandy
170g / 6oz Cashel Blue
cheese, crumbled
½ tsp black pepper
Salt to taste
Grated nutmeg to garnish

Method:

1. Boil the potatoes in their jackets until they are tender. Peel and mash while they are hot.
2. While the potatoes are cooking, heat the oil and butter in a heavy-bottomed sauté pan. Add the onions and sauté until they are caramelised (should take about 20–30 minutes over a low heat). Add the garlic and sauté until fragrant. Add the brandy to the pan, and sauté to reduce the liquid by half. Stir in the herbs and pepper. Remove from the heat.
3. Add the butter, cream and cheese to the potatoes. Add the onion / herb mixture and stir to blend. Sprinkle the top with ¼ tsp of nutmeg.

4. Fill an ovenproof dish with potatoes. With a fork, create a design on top of the potatoes. Broil until the top is golden brown (should take about 5 minutes).

This can be made in advance, chilled, and baked to re-heat.

Champ

Serves 6

7 medium to large boiling potatoes, unpeeled
5–6 scallions
55g / 2oz butter, more if desired
100ml / 4 fluid oz milk, plus more if needed

Method:

1. Place the potatoes in a large pot, cover with cold water and bring to the boil. Pour off all but 2 inches of water, cover with a lid, and reduce the heat to low. Cook for 25 minutes or until a skewer will easily pass through the potato.
2. While the potatoes are cooking, chop the scallions and bring to the boil in milk. Remove from the heat and let the scallions sit in the hot milk.
3. Peel the potatoes while they are hot. Place them in a mixing bowl and mash with a mixer or potato masher. Add the butter, milk and scallions.

Season with some salt and pepper and keep warm until needed.

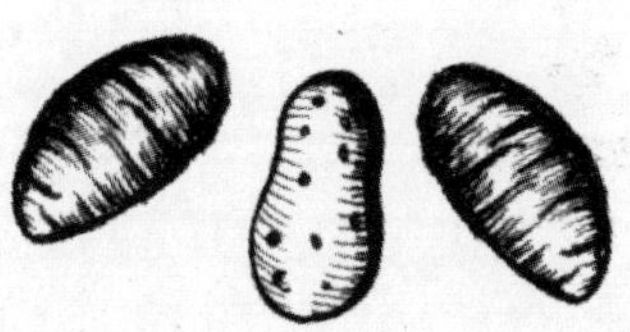

Chinese Pot Stickers – Steamed & Fried Dumplings

Makes 18 dumplings

Pot sticker dough

115g / 4oz strong white flour
100ml / 4 fluid oz boiling water

Dough method:

1. Put the flour into a bowl. Gradually stir in hot water with a fork.
2. When combined remove the dough from the bowl and knead until smooth (about 5 minutes).
3. Put back into bowl, cover with a damp towel and allow to rest for 20 minutes.
4. Remove from bowl, knead for 5 minutes and roll into a 9x1-inch tube. Cut into 18 pieces; roll out into 2½-inch pancakes. Keep covered with damp towel.

Filling

1 small York cabbage
1 small onion, chopped fine
1 tsp minced fresh ginger
1 tbsp soy sauce
1 tbsp dry white wine
225g / 8oz pork sausage meat
½ tsp salt
Pinch of dry mustard

Filling method:

1. Finely chop the cabbage leaves then sprinkle them with salt

to help remove excess moisture. Squeeze in a dish towel. Combine the cabbage, onion, ginger, soy sauce, wine, sausage meat, salt and mustard in a bowl. Mix them together well.

2. Place 1 tbsp of the mixture in the centre of each dumpling and fold in half. Wet the edges with water to seal and pinch closed. Stand on the folded edge – the top should be round and the bottom should be flat.
3. Place 1 tbsp of oil in a frying pan. Add the pot stickers and fry until they are golden (about 2 minutes). Pour in 150ml / 6 fluid oz of water, cover and steam for 12 minutes. Uncover and cook for 2 further minutes to evaporate the rest of the water.

Serve while warm with dipping sauce.

Dipping Sauce

75ml / 3 fluid oz soy sauce
25ml / 1 fluid oz rice vinegar
1 tsp sesame oil
1 tbsp soft brown sugar
1 finely chopped scallion
Dash of chilli oil

Dipping Sauce method:

Mix the ingredients together in a small bowl. Serve in small dishes as a dip for pot stickers.

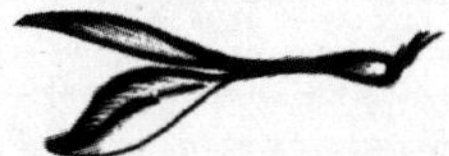

Cornbread Stuffing

Serves 6–8
Preheat oven to 180C (350F)

Cornbread

225g / 8oz strong white flour
55g / 2oz caster sugar
4 tsps baking powder
¾ tsp salt
225g / 8oz cornmeal (maize meal)
2 eggs
200ml / 8 fluid oz milk
50ml / 2 fluid oz sunflower oil

Cornbread method:

1. Combine all of the dry ingredients in a bowl, and make a well in the centre of the mix.
2. Combine the milk, eggs, and oil in a measuring jug and pour into the well in the dry ingredients. Mix with a spoon and pour the batter into an oiled 8x8-inch baking pan. Bake for 25 minutes or until a tester inserted in the centre comes out clean.The bread should be made the day before needed for stuffing as day-old bread works best.

Stuffing Seasoning mix

2 tsps salt
1½ tsps white pepper
1 tsp cayenne
1 tsp dried oregano
½ tsp thyme
2 tsps rubbed sage

Stuffing method:

Combine in small bowl and set aside.

Vegetable mixture

115g / 4oz butter
4 tbsps sunflower oil
170g / 6oz onions, finely chopped
170g / 6oz green bell pepper, finely chopped
115g / 4oz celery, finely chopped
1 tbsp garlic, minced
2 bay leaves
340g / 12oz chicken livers, cooked and diced
200ml / 8 fluid oz chicken stock
1 tsp Tabasco sauce
50ml / 2 fluid oz dry white wine
750g / 28oz finely crumbled cornbread
1 330ml / 13 fluid oz can evaporated milk
3 eggs, beaten

Vegetable method:

1. In a large sauté pan combine the butter and oil. Melt together over a medium heat and add the vegetables along with the garlic and bay leaves. Sauté the mix until the vegetables are tender. Add the seasoning and cook for 5 minutes. Remove the bay leaves, then stir in the chicken livers, stock, wine and Tabasco, and cook for an additional 5 minutes.
2. Remove from the heat, pour into a large mixing bowl, and add the cornbread, milk, and eggs, stirring all the time to combine.

3. Spoon the mix into an oiled 13x9-inch baking dish, bake at 180C (350F) for 35–40 minutes or until golden brown.

Serve with turkey or chicken.

My mother always put the stuffing together the day before, using day-old cornbread, allowing the flavours to marry. The glorious smell of turkey and stuffing takes me back to my childhood instantly.

Stuffing with Sausage

Makes about 1300ml / 50 fluid oz

1 tbsp butter
1 medium onion, chopped
2 shallots, minced
225g / 8oz seasoned sausage meat
115g / 4oz soft breadcrumbs
115g / 4oz panko / Japanese breadcrumbs
100ml / 4 fluid oz chicken broth
1 Granny Smith apple, peeled, cored and diced
6 mushrooms, chopped
2 stalks celery, chopped
50ml / 2 fluid oz brandy
2 tbsps dry white wine
1 tbsp parsley, minced
1 tsp thyme leaves, chopped
Pinch of ground allspice
1 tsp black pepper / salt to taste

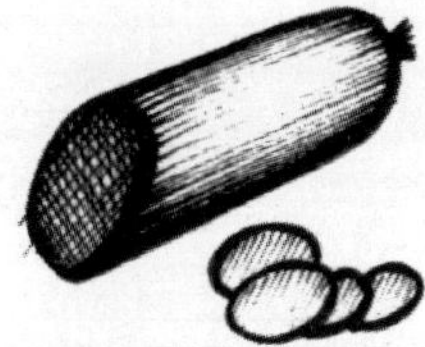

Method:

1. Melt the butter in a large sauté pan over a medium heat. Add the onions, shallot, and celery and sauté them until soft. Add the crumbled sausage meat and cook until it is browned.
2. Add the mushrooms and wine. Sauté until the mushrooms are soft. Remove from the heat and let cool.
3. Combine the breadcrumbs, panko, spices, herbs, sausage/ vegetable mixture, and apple in a large bowl. Moisten the mix with broth and brandy.
4. Cool the stuffing completely before using. Stuff the poultry or bake in a covered dish.

Quick Corn Salad

Serves 4

400–455g / 14–16oz can of corn, drained
340g / 12oz canned jalapenos, drained and chopped
40g / 1½oz chopped red onion
115g / 4oz chopped red bell pepper
2 tbsps chopped fresh basil
1 tbsp chopped cilantro

Dressing

1½ tbsps rioja red wine vinegar
1 tbsp olive oil
½ tsp cumin
Salt and pepper to taste

Method:

1. Combine the salad ingredients in a bowl. Prepare the salad dressing in a small bowl and add to the salad. Cover and chill.

Serve as a garnish or as a salad.

Jansson's Temptation Potatoes

Serves 4
Preheat oven to 200C (400F)

6 medium rooster potatoes, peeled
2 medium onions, sliced thinly
1 can anchovies, drained
2 tbsps panko / Japanese breadcrumbs
3 tbsps butter
150ml / 6 fluid oz cream
170g / 6oz Emmental cheese, grated
1 tbsp fresh parsley, chopped
1 tsp black pepper

Method:

1. Cut the potatoes into ¼-inch matchsticks and place them into a bowl of cold water until needed.
2. Sauté the onions in butter until soft – do not brown. Season with salt and pepper.
3. Drain and towel dry the potatoes.
4. Layer the potatoes, cheese, onion, and anchovies into a baking dish. Repeat the process using up all of the ingredients, ending with a potato layer. Sprinkle with some panko, and then pour cream over the mixture. Bake until the potatoes are tender and the liquid has been absorbed (about 50 minutes). Cover with foil to keep the potatoes warm.

Marinated Carrots

Serves 6–8

455g / 16oz carrots,
slice diagonally ¼-inch thick
50ml / 2 fluid oz olive oil
2 tbsps red wine vinegar
2 cloves garlic, minced fine
1 tbsp fresh lemon juice
1 tbsp parsley, minced
1 tsp Dijon mustard
1 tsp caster sugar
Salt and pepper to taste

Method:

1. Cover the carrots with cold water in a medium saucepan. Bring to the boil, cook until the carrots are crisp, but tender. Drain and plunge the carrots into a bowl of ice water to stop the cooking process.
2. In a small bowl, combine the vinegar, garlic, lemon juice, parsley, Dijon mustard, and sugar. Stir the ingredients to combine them and then whisk in the oil.
3. Drain the carrots and pat them dry on some kitchen paper. Pour on the dressing and stir to coat. Add some salt and pepper if desired. Cover and chill for at least 2 hours.

Serve at room temperature.

Sweet Onion & Prosciutto Bread Pudding

Serves 6–8
Preheat oven to 190C (375F)

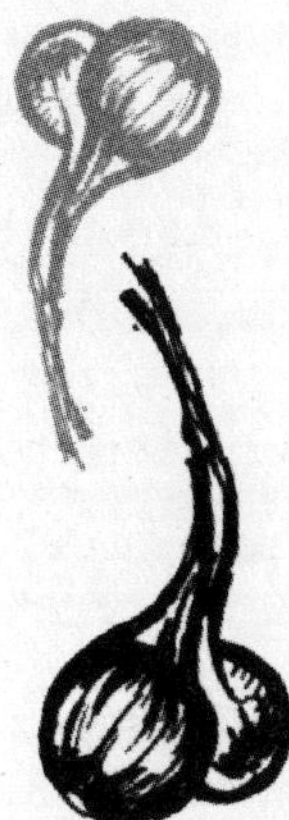

100ml / 4 fluid oz milk
225g / 8oz day-old bread, cut into ½-inch cubes
1 tbsp olive oil
1 small sweet onion, chopped fine
1 clove garlic, minced
115g / 4oz mushrooms, chopped fine
1 Granny Smith apple, peeled, cored and diced
2 tsps thyme, chopped
1 tsp sage, chopped
Pinch of nutmeg
2 slices prosciutto, chopped fine
2 tbsps brandy
3 egg yolks, beaten
½ tsp salt
¼ tsp black pepper

Method:

1. Lightly oil 6–8 ramekins or a 7x11-inch ovenproof dish.
2. Warm the milk, but do not let boil. Put the bread into a large bowl, then pour the milk over the bread, stirring to mix. Let it soak for 20 minutes, stirring occasionally to ensure that the bread gets soaked through.
3. Pour some oil into a heavy-bottomed sauté pan. When the oil is hot add the onions and sauté for 5 minutes. Add the garlic, and sauté until fragrant; add the apple, mushrooms,

thyme, sage, nutmeg, and prosciutto. Reduce the heat to low and cook just until the apple begins to soften.

4. Add the brandy and cook for 2–3 more minutes to release the flavours. Remove from the heat and allow to cool.
5. Combine the onion mixture with the soaked bread. Add the eggs, salt and pepper, and stir well to distribute the ingredients.
6. Spoon into baking dishes; add the boiling water to come half-way up the sides of the dishes.
7. Bake for 40–60 minutes or until a knife blade inserted in the pudding comes out clean.

This dish can be prepared to baking stage and refrigerated until it is ready to bake. Make sure to bring it to room temperature before baking. It makes a perfect accompaniment to Sirloin Steak with Peppercorn Cognac Sauce (see page 114)

Dips & Tasty Bits

Crab & Artichoke Dip

Preheat oven to 200C (400F)

55g / 2oz cream cheese, room temperature
100ml / 4 fluid oz mayonnaise, preferably homemade
115g / 4oz crabmeat
140g / 5oz freshly grated Parmesan cheese
3 455g / 16oz cans artichoke hearts, drained and chopped
1 scallion, chopped fine
1 tbsp fresh parsley, chopped fine
1½ tsps white wine vinegar
½ tsp Tabasco sauce
½ tsp Beau Monde seasoning
1 tsp fresh lemon juice

Method:

1. Beat the cream cheese with an electric mixer until it is light and fluffy. Add the mayonnaise and beat to combine. Fold in the remaining ingredients with a spatula.
2. Place the mixture into individual ramekins or into a baking dish and bake for 15 minutes.

Serve immediately with some Melba toast or small brown bread slices.

Homemade Mayonnaise

2 fresh eggs
¾ tsp sea salt
¼ tsp dry mustard
Pinch of cayenne pepper
25ml / 1 fluid oz freshly squeezed lemon juice
200ml / 8 fluid oz olive oil
200ml / 8 fluid oz sunflower oil

Method:

1. Put the egg, salt, mustard, cayenne, and lemon juice in a food processor or blender. Combine.
2. Combine the oils in a measuring jug with a pour spout. Turn on the processor or blender and begin adding the oils in a fine slow steady drizzle until the mixture begins to thicken. Continue adding oil in a steady stream until all the oil is completely used. Chill until needed.

If the mixture is too thick add a few drops of hot water to thin it.

Marinated Goat Cheese

Serves 8

50ml / 2 fluid oz olive oil
200ml / 8 fluid oz white
balsamic vinegar
28g / 1oz fresh thyme leaves
2 tbsps chopped fresh rosemary
¼ tsp salt
¼ tsp black peppercorns
¼ tsp red peppercorns
455g / 16oz firm goat cheese, cubed

Method:

1. Combine the oil, vinegar, herbs and spices in a kiln jar. Allow to set for 7 days in a fridge in order to allow the flavours to combine.
2. Add the cheese. Chill for 2 hours before serving.

Serve as part of antipasto, or as garnish to a salad.

Marinated Olives

170g / 6oz canned black olives,
pitted and drained
50ml / 2 fluid oz olive oil
2 tbsps chopped oregano
2 tbsps chopped basil
2 cloves garlic, minced
1 tbsp balsamic vinegar
½ tsp red chilli flakes

Method:

1. Combine all of the ingredients in a large jar with a tight-fitting lid. Shake well, then refrigerate overnight to allow the flavours to combine.

Keeps for 2 weeks in a fridge.

Pickled Green Beans

Makes about 2 litres / 64 fluid oz

900g / 32oz long green beans
4 tsps pickling spice
4 cloves garlic
1 tsp chilli seeds
500ml / 20 fluid oz white wine vinegar
500ml / 20 fluid oz water
55g / 2oz pickling salt

Method:

1. Wash and trim the green beans. Do not use any with blemishes. Put them lengthwise into sterile pint kilner jars. Put 1 clove garlic, ¼ tsp chilli seeds, and 1 tsp pickling spice into each jar.
2. Pour the water, vinegar, and pickling salt into a large pot. Bring to boil, remove from the heat and pour into the jars, leaving a ¼-inch space at the top of each jar. Wipe the tops and close the lids. Place the jars into a large saucepan and cover with hot water. Place the lid on the pot and bring to the boil over a high heat. Boil for 10 minutes.
3. Remove from the pot, then let stand for 2 hours to cool. Store for at least 2 months in a dark, cool place before using.

Serve as a garnish to seafood salads, tomato juice, tarts and quiche.

Onion Marmalade

Makes about 340g / 12ozs

50ml / 2 fluid oz olive oil
455g / 16oz sweet onions, diced
3 cloves garlic, minced
50ml / 2 fluid oz balsamic vinegar
55g / 2oz soft brown sugar
2 tbsps sun-dried tomato puree
½ tsp ground ginger
¼ tsp ground cloves
¼ tsp ground nutmeg
¼ tsp coarsely ground black pepper
½ tsp sea salt
2 tbsps bourbon
¼ tsp dry mustard

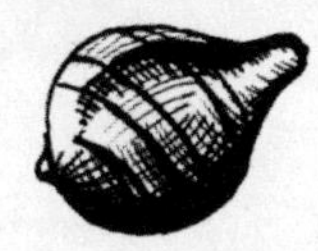

Method:

1. Heat the oil in a heavy-bottomed sauté pan. Sauté the onions and garlic until they are soft and just starting to brown. Add the vinegar and brown sugar and cook for 5 minutes. Add the rest of the ingredients and simmer until thick, stirring frequently to prevent scorching.
2. Pour into a sterile jar and refrigerate until needed. Serve warmed or at room temperature.

Great with pork, steak, or as an accompaniment to cheese.

Spicy Vegetarian Chilli

Serves 8

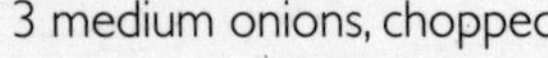

3 medium onions, chopped
2 medium green bell peppers, chopped
4 stalks celery, chopped
4 cloves garlic, minced
2 tbsps sunflower oil
2 800g / 28oz cans chopped
tomatoes, undrained

2 430g / 15oz cans red kidney beans
1 430g / 15oz can cannellini beans
1 430g / 15oz can black beans
1 300ml / 12 fluid oz can of beer
1 tsp thyme
1 tsp cumin
50ml / 2 fluid oz red wine vinegar

1 bay leaf
1 tbsp chilli powder
1 tbsp chopped parsley
1½ tsps dried basil
1½ tsps dried oregano
½ tsp pepper
Salt to taste

Method:

1. Heat the oil in a large pot; add the onions, green peppers, celery, and garlic. Sauté until tender.
2. Add the tomatoes, undrained beans, beer, vinegar, herbs and spices. Cover with a lid and simmer for 1 hour.
3. Remove the lid and simmer for another hour. Serve.
4. Garnish with grated cheddar cheese, sour cream, or guacamole.

Serve with Cheddar Pepper Bread (see page 148). Non-vegetarians will love this chilli!

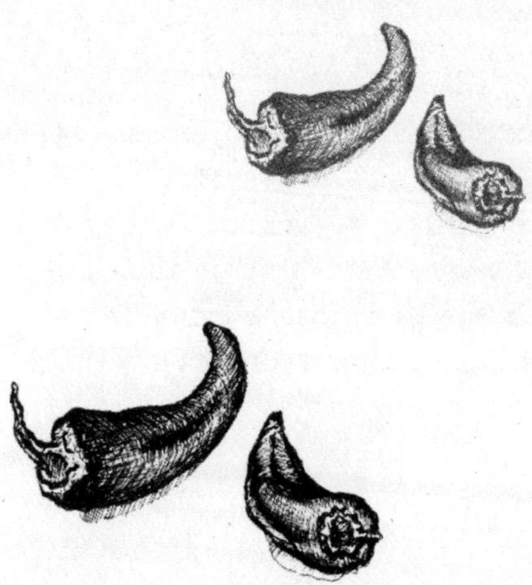

Courgette Pancakes

Serves 6
Preheat oven to 180C (350F)

455g / 16oz grated un-peeled courgettes
55g / 2oz self-raising flour
55g / 2oz grated Parmesan cheese
1 egg, lightly beaten
1 tsp finely chopped shallot
¼ tsp black pepper
½ tsp salt
2 tbsps butter
1 tbsp oil
6 tbsps grated cheddar cheese

Method:

1. Combine the courgette, flour, Parmesan, egg, shallot, salt and pepper.
2. Melt the butter and oil in a non-stick pan. Drop in the batter by tbsp and cook until it is golden. Turn and repeat.
3. Remove to a baking sheet and sprinkle with 1 tbsp of cheddar on top. Place into a hot oven to melt the cheese.

Serve as a light lunch or as a side vegetable.

Meat

Sirloin Steak with Peppercorn Cognac Sauce

Serves 4–6

Peppercorn Cognac Sauce

1 tbsp butter
2 tbsps minced shallots
1 tbsp crushed green peppercorns
100ml / 4 fluid oz dry red wine
2 tbsps cognac
400ml / 16 fluid oz cream
½ tsp dry mustard
400ml / 16 fluid oz beef stock, reduced to 100ml / 4 fluid oz

Method:

1. Melt the butter in a sauté pan. Add the shallots and peppercorns and sauté until golden.
2. Increase the heat to high. Add the wine and cognac and boil until reduced to about 50ml / 2 fluid oz. Add the reduced stock and cream. Boil until it is reduced to a sauce consistency (should take about 5 minutes).
3. Stir in the dry mustard and season to taste.
4. Grill the steaks and serve with the sauce spooned over the top.

Serve with Sweet Onion and Prosciutto Bread Pudding (see page 101) and steamed asparagus.

All-American Meat Loaf

Serves 4–6
Preheat oven to 170C (325F)

455g / 16oz lean ground beef
225g / 8oz pork sausage meat
50ml / 2 fluid oz ketchup
plus extra for garnish
1 tbsp HP sauce (or steak
sauce of choice)
1½ tsps Worcestershire sauce
1 tsp Tabasco sauce
2 tsps chilli powder
1 tsp black pepper
½ tsp salt
55g / 2oz green bell pepper, chopped fine
1 medium onion, chopped fine
55g / 2oz celery, chopped fine
1 egg, beaten
225g / 8oz panko / Japanese
bread crumbs

Method:

1. Combine the beef and pork in a large bowl. Mix the ketchup, HP sauce, Worcestershire and Tabasco with the spices in a small bowl. Add the chopped vegetables, panko, egg, and sauce mixture to the meat. Stir well to combine and put into a loaf pan or ovenproof pan. Drizzle the top with ketchup and bake for 1 hour.

Serve with fluffy mashed potatoes. Use any leftovers to make delicious sandwiches.

Asian Roasted Pork Loin

Serves 6–8
Preheat oven to 170C (325F)

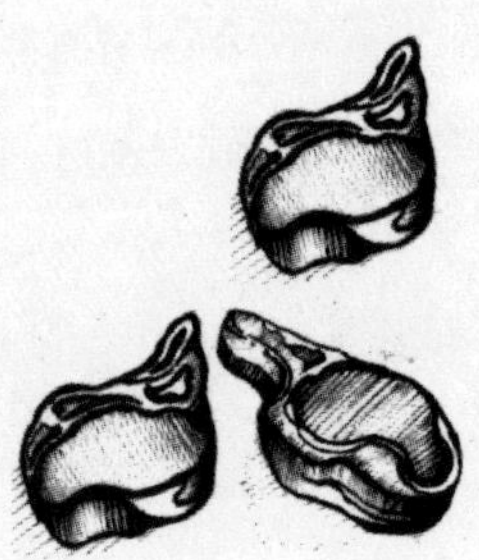

100ml / 4 fluid oz soy sauce
50ml / 2 fluid oz sunflower oil
2 tbsps black treacle
1 tbsp ground ginger
2 tsps ground mustard
4 cloves garlic, minced
50ml / 2 fluid oz orange juice, freshly squeezed
1800–2200g / 64–80oz rolled boneless pork loin roast

Method:

1. Whisk the marinade ingredients together and set aside.
2. Place the roast on a cutting board and butterfly.
3. Place the roast in a shallow dish and pour the marinade over it. Cover and refrigerate for 8 hours.
4. Remove the meat from marinade, and keep the marinade to one side. Tie the roast and place into a roasting pan. Bake at 170C (325F) for 2 hours. Brush with the marinade every half-hour.

Serve with basmati rice or boiled potatoes.

Beef Tenderloin Steak with Red Wine Sauce

Serves 4

4 beef tenderloin steaks (use approx. 170–225g / 6–8oz per person)
4–8 slices streaky rashers of bacon
2 tbs freshly cracked black pepper
Salt to taste
55g / 2oz butter
2 shallots, chopped
2 cloves garlic, chopped
2 slices onion
1 small carrot, sliced
2 sprigs parsley
1 tsp black peppercorns
2 cloves
2 bay leaves
2 tbsps flour
250ml / 10 fluid oz beef bouillon
200ml / 8 fluid oz red wine

Method:

1. Begin by preparing the sauce. Heat the butter in a sauté pan, then add the shallots, garlic, onions, carrot, herbs, and spices. Sauté until the onions are soft (about 5 minutes).
2. Stir in the flour and cook for a few minutes to begin a roux. Add the bouillon and red wine. Stir well, reduce the heat and allow to simmer for 20–30 minutes.
3. Strain the sauce into a saucepan and set aside until needed.
4. Wrap the bacon around the outer sides of the steak and secure with a cocktail stick. Dredge the surface of the steaks

with cracked pepper and sprinkle with salt. Grill or broil the steaks as desired and serve with heated sauce. The sauce can be made ahead of time and frozen for later use.

Serve with potato of choice.

Bourbon Pork Chops

Serves 2
Preheat oven to 200C (400F)

2 boneless 1½-inch thick pork loin chops
2 tbsps demerara brown sugar
400ml / 16 fluid oz apple juice, boiled to reduce to 110ml / 4 fluid oz
1½ tsp Dijon mustard
2 tbsps bourbon (no substitutes)
1 tsp lemon zest
¼ tsp cayenne pepper
2 tbsps apple cider vinegar
¼ tsp rubbed sage

Method:

1. Combine the marinade ingredients in a casserole dish. Add the pork chops; turn over in the marinade to coat. Cover and leave for 2 hours, turn over and leave for another 2 hours. The meat can be marinated for longer if more flavour is required.
2. Remove the meat from the marinade. Grill or pan sear for 4–6 minutes per side, transfer to an oven and finish cooking for 10 minutes at 200C (400F).
3. While the meat is in the oven boil the marinade to reduce, then drizzle over the cooked chops.

Serve with Champ (see page 91)

Mojito Pork Loin Chops with Sautéed York Cabbage

Serves 2

Preheat oven to 200C (400F)

2 1½-inch thick boneless pork loin chops

1 head of York cabbage

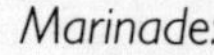

Marinade:

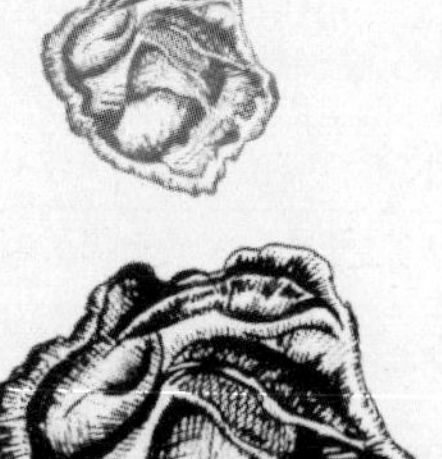

50ml / 2 fluid oz olive oil

50ml / 2 fluid oz freshly squeezed orange juice

2 tbsps freshly squeezed lime juice

2 tbsps soy sauce

1 tsp cumin

1 tsp chilli flakes

2 tsps dried oregano

2 tsps smoked paprika

4 scallions, chopped

Method:

1. Combine the marinade ingredients, pour over the chops, cover and refrigerate for 2 hours.
2. Grill the chops for 10 minutes, turning twice. Finish cooking the chops in an oven for 10 minutes or as desired.
3. Boil the marinade for 5 minutes and drizzle over the chops. Serve with sautéed York cabbage.

Cabbage method:

Remove the outer leaves and wash thoroughly. Cut the spine away from all but the tender centre leaves. Roll up the leaves a few at a time and julienne. Sauté in a pan with some melted butter until tender, then season with salt and pepper to taste. Do not cover with a lid (it will take the green colour away) and do not sauté until too soft. Serve the chop on a bed of cabbage with a drizzle of sauce.

Serve with Champ (see page 91)

Poultry

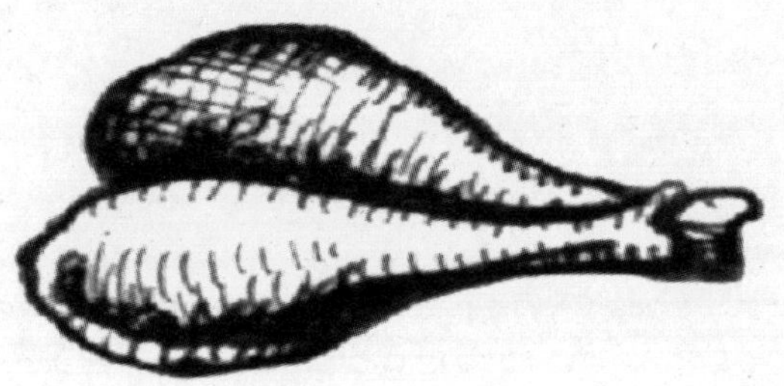

Duck Breast with Balsamic Glaze

Serves 2
Preheat oven to 200C (400F)

2 duck breasts
Sea salt
1–2 tbsps quality balsamic vinegar
50ml / 2 fluid oz Madeira wine
100ml / 4 fluid oz chicken stock
1 tsp corn flour
1 tbsp brandy

Method:

1. Score the skin of the duck breasts with a criss-cross pattern. Sprinkle liberally with salt, then allow to rest for half an hour.
2. Heat a heavy frying pan until hot, then add the breasts skin side down and cook until browned. Turn the breasts over and cook the flesh side until it is browned. This will take between 5 and 10 minutes per side. Remove to a baking dish and place into the oven to finish cooking.
3. Pour off all but 1 tbsp of fat from the skillet and de-glaze with 50ml / 2 fluid oz Madeira. Add 1–2 tbsps of balsamic vinegar and reduce by half. Add 100ml / 4 fluid oz of chicken stock and bring to the boil. Mix 1 tsp of corn flour with 1 tsp water, and whisk into a broth mixture. Allow to thicken and add a splash of brandy (about 1 tbsp). Boil again, season and spoon over the duck to serve.

Serve with Champ (see page 91).

Chicken Breast Abbeyside

Serves 4
Preheat oven to 200C (400F)

4 chicken breasts, boned and skinned
225g / 8oz mozzarella
cheese, sliced thin
115g / 4oz salami, sliced thin
2 tbsps parsley, chopped fine
2 eggs, beaten
225g / 8oz dry breadcrumbs
3 tbsps butter
3 tbsps olive oil

Sauce

50ml / 2 fluid oz dry white wine
100ml / 4 fluid oz chicken stock
1 tbsp lemon juice
¼ tsp black pepper
2 tsps chopped parsley

Chicken method:

1. Flatten the chicken breasts to ¼-inch. Place 2–3 slices of salami and cheese on half of each breast. Fold over and secure with cocktail sticks.
2. Mix the parsley with the breadcrumbs. Dip the chicken packet into the egg and breadcrumbs mixture.
3. Melt the butter with oil, and fry the breaded breast until it is golden. Turn the chicken over and repeat. Remove to a baking dish, and place in an oven for 10 minutes to finish cooking.

Sauce method:

De-glaze the pan with white wine. Boil to reduce the wine by half, then add the stock and lemon juice. Boil down to reduce, and add the parsley and pepper. Pour over the chicken to serve. Garnish with lemon slices.

Serve with boiled baby potatoes and green beans.

Chinese Chicken Wings

Preheat oven to 180C (350F)

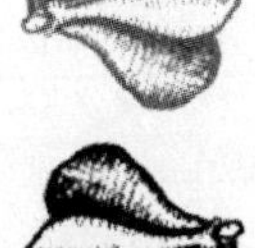

900g / 32oz chicken wings
1 clove garlic, minced
100ml / 4 fluid oz soy sauce
100ml / 4 fluid oz honey
2 tbsps bourbon
2 tbsps fresh lemon juice
1 tbsp dry mustard
¼ tsp ground ginger
Pinch of cayenne
Sesame seeds to garnish

Method:

1. Separate the chicken wings at the joints. Cut off the wing tips and discard. This will give you one tiny wing and one tiny leg.
2. Warm the honey and whisk in the soy sauce, whiskey, lemon juice and spices. Place the wing pieces into a ceramic dish and pour the marinade over them. Cover and refrigerate overnight or for at least 6 hours.
3. Discard the marinade and place the wing pieces onto a baking sheet. Bake until browned (for about 10 minutes), then turn over and bake the other side. The wings can be grilled/broiled but must be watched closely as the honey burns quickly.

To serve place on serving dish and sprinkle with sesame seeds.

Chicken Breast Piccata

Serves 4
Preheat oven to 180C (350F)

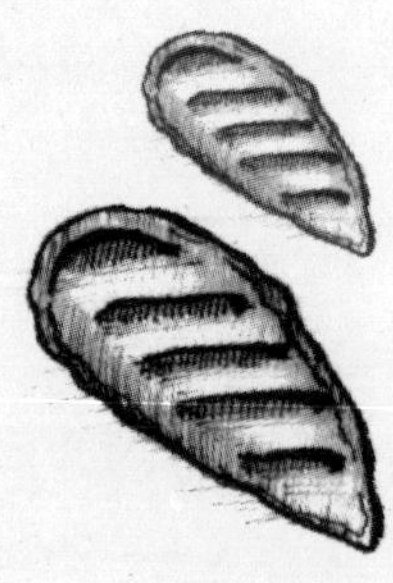

2 whole chicken breasts, skin, bone, and cut into half
115g / 4oz flour, seasoned with salt and pepper
75ml / 3 fluid oz sunflower oil
200ml / 8 fluid oz dry white wine
2 tbsps drained and rinsed capers
115g / 4oz butter, no substitutes, cut into pieces and kept cold
Juice of ½ lemon
Chopped fresh parsley
Cooked linguini, kept warm – allow 115g / 4oz per serving
4 slices paper-thin Parma ham

Method:

1. Line a baking sheet with some parchment, place the Parma slices onto paper and put into a hot oven until crispy (for about 1–2 minutes). Set aside until ready to serve.
2. Place each chicken breast between 2 sheets of cling film. Flatten to ¼-inch thickness; be careful not to tear the meat.
3. Dredge the breasts in seasoned flour and shake off any excess flour.
4. Heat the oil in a heavy-bottomed sauté pan. Sauté the breasts for about 1 minute on each side, or until golden brown. Remove to a baking sheet and keep warm in an oven while preparing the sauce.
5. Pour off the oil from the pan, de-glaze with some wine, and scrape up the browned bits. Boil until the mixture has been

reduced by half. Remove from heat, then whisk in the butter, one piece at a time. Keep warm. Do not let the sauce get too hot or it will turn liquid and will not emulsify. Stir in the lemon juice and capers.

6. Bring a large pot of water with 1 tsp of salt to a full boil. Add the pasta and cook until it is firm, yet tender. Drain, rinse in warm water, drain again and toss with 1 tsp of olive oil. When serving, place a bed of linguini onto a warmed plate, lay the chicken onto the pasta and pour the sauce over the top.

Finish with a slice of Parma ham.

Fish

Cod Grecian

Serves 2
Preheat oven to 200C (400F)

Cod (allow 170g / 6oz per serving)
Flour
55g / 2oz butter
1 small onion, sliced thin
115g / 4oz sliced mushrooms
1 clove garlic, minced
1 lemon
150ml / 6 fluid oz dry white wine
4 tbsps feta cheese, crumbled
1 tsp Pernod liqueur
6 plum tomatoes, peeled, seeded, and diced
4 tbsps tomato paste
4 scallions, thinly sliced
8 black olives, pitted

Method:

1. Skin and bone the cod. Cut into 2 serving pieces. Dust each piece with flour and shake to remove any excess.
2. Heat the butter in a sauté pan. Brown the fish on each side and remove to a baking dish. Bake for 10 minutes to finish cooking. This may take more or less time depending on the thickness of the cod.
3. Melt the butter in the sauté pan. Add the sliced onion, mushrooms, garlic, and juice of ½ lemon. Sauté until the onions are soft, then add the wine and feta. Cook just until the cheese melts, then add the Pernod.
4. Add the diced tomatoes, olives, tomato paste, and stir to

combine. Add the scallions and remove the mixture from the heat.

5. Spoon the sauce onto a warmed plate, then place the fish onto the sauce and garnish with a lemon slice.

This dish is lovely served with orzo (rice-shaped pasta). Allow 28g / 1oz uncooked orzo per serving. Bring 1 quart of water with ½ tsp of salt to a full boil. Add 55g / 2oz orzo and cook for 10–14 minutes or until tender but still firm Drain, rinse and toss with 1 tsp of olive oil. Re-warm in a skillet and toss with fresh finely minced parsley and 1 tsp olive oil.

Crab Cakes with Rémoulade Sauce

Serves 4
Preheat oven to 130C (250F)

4–5 slices white bread, crust removed
2 tbsps red bell pepper, chopped fine
50ml / 2 fluid oz mayonnaise (homemade preferred)

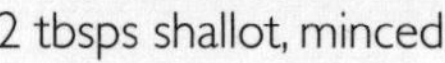
1 large egg, beaten
2 tbsps shallot, minced
2 tbsps parsley, minced
2 tbsps lemon juice, fresh

1 tsp Dijon mustard
¼ tsp cayenne pepper
¼–½ tsp Old Bay seasoning or other spicy seafood seasoning

455g / 16oz fresh crabmeat
55g / 2oz butter, no substitutions
4 tbsps oil

Crab cakes method:

1. Make the breadcrumbs by pulsing the bread in a food processor. Soft crumbs versus powder are preferred.
2. Combine the mayonnaise, egg, shallots, parsley, Old Bay seasoning, cayenne, lemon juice, mustard and red bell pepper in a medium size mixing bowl. Fold in the crab and 225g / 8oz of the breadcrumbs until just blended.
3. Line a baking sheet with parchment. Place remaining bread crumbs onto a large plate. Using a round cup fill with crab mixture and turn out onto the breadcrumbs. Shape gently into a ½-inch round, coating each one with the crumbs.

Transfer to the baking sheet. Repeat the process using all of the crab mixture, then refrigerate for 4 hours.

4. Prepare clarified butter by melting the butter in a measuring jug, then let stand a few minutes, skim off the foamy top and discard. Pour the clear liquid into a cup and discard any milky solids that fall to the bottom.
5. Heat 1 tbsp of clarified butter and 2 tbsps of oil in a frying pan over a medium heat. Add 4 crab cakes and cook until golden (about 4 minutes), turn over and repeat. Transfer to a baking sheet and keep warm in the oven. Wipe the frying pan with kitchen paper, and repeat the process.

Rémoulade Sauce:

200ml / 8 fluid oz mayonnaise
– homemade is preferred
55g / 2oz Dijon mustard with seeds
55g / 2oz minced celery
55g / 2oz minced oil-packed
sun dried tomatoes
2 tbsps minced red bell pepper
2 tbsps minced shallot
1 tbsp minced red onion
1 tbsp minced parsley
1 tbsp sweet paprika
½ tsp salt
¼ tsp white pepper
1 tsp grated horseradish sauce

Combine all of the ingredients in a bowl and mix well. Taste, and adjust seasoning if necessary. Chill until needed.

Rémoulade can be made a few days in advance and is great with any fish.

Sea Bass Marinara

Serves 2
Preheat oven to 200C (400F)

1 sea bass – skinned, filleted
2 tbsps olive oil
1 clove garlic, minced
1 tbsp parsley, chopped
1 tsp sugar
½ tsp salt
¼ tsp dried basil leaves
½ tsp dried oregano leaves
Pinch of black pepper
Pinch of cayenne
455g / 16oz can chopped tomatoes with juice

Method:

1. Prepare the sauce: heat 1 tbsp of oil in a sauté pan, then add the garlic and sauté until golden brown. Discard the garlic. Add the parsley, sugar, salt, herbs, spices, and tomatoes. Bring to boil, reduce heat and simmer for 20–30 minutes, stirring occasionally. If the sauce becomes too dry add some water or a little white wine.
2. In the frying pan, heat 1 tbsp of oil. Season the fish with salt and pepper. Place the fish onto a hot frying pan and sear until golden, then turn over and repeat. Test by flaking with a fork. Put the fish onto warmed plates and spoon the sauce over the fish. Garnish with some minced parsley.

Serve with orzo, basmati rice, or with parsley-buttered boiled baby potatoes.

Helvic Head Seafood Gumbo

Serves 8–10
Preheat oven to 180C (350F)

Roux

150ml / 6 fluid oz sunflower oil
225g / 8oz strong white flour

Gumbo

2 tbsps butter
455g / 16oz finely chopped onions
455g / 16oz finely chopped green bell peppers
455g / 16oz finely chopped celery
225g / 8oz finely chopped red bell pepper
3 cloves garlic, minced
455g / 16oz smoked sausage, cut into ½-inch cubes
½ tsp dried oregano
½ tsp dried thyme
2 bay leaves
½ tsp cayenne pepper
½ tsp black pepper
2– 455g / 16oz canned tomatoes, drained
1200ml / 48 fluid oz fish or chicken stock
200ml / 8 fluid oz dry white wine
285g / 10oz crabmeat
675g / 24oz chicken breast, skinned, boned, cut into 1-inch cubes

1 kg / 35oz shelled Dublin Bay prawns
310g / 11oz okra, cut into
½-inch pieces
400g / 16oz basmati rice
600ml / 24 fluid oz water
1 tsp salt

Method:

1. Prepare the roux: heat a heavy-bottomed pan over a medium heat, then pour in the oil and flour. Whisk to combine, and cook until the flour becomes a dark brick-red. Whisk constantly to prevent scorching. This should take about 10 to 20 minutes and is essential to the taste of the gumbo. If the mixture burns or scorches discard and start over – the burnt flavour will ruin the gumbo.
2. Heat the butter in a large sauté pan. Add the onions, peppers, celery and garlic. Sauté over a medium heat until the vegetables are soft.
3. Put the vegetables, sausage, spices, tomatoes, stock and wine into a large pot. Bring to the boil and simmer for 30 minutes. Stir in the roux and cook for 1 hour. Add the chicken pieces and cook for another 30 minutes.
4. Add the okra and cook until it is just tender (about 10 minutes). Do not overcook, or the okra will become quite slimy.
5. Add the crab and prawns, then cook for 2–5 minutes or until cooked through.
6. This is not an overly spiced gumbo; Tabasco can be added to increase the 'heat'.

Rice method:

1. Boil the water and add salt. Rinse the rice and place into an ovenproof dish with a tight lid. Add the boiled water, stir, and cover with kitchen foil. Put a lid over the foil and bake for 45 minutes. Remove from the oven and fluff with a fork. Rice will stay hot sitting covered in a pan for 15–30 minutes.

Serve in large pasta bowls with a scoop of rice in the centre.

I traditionally serve gumbo on New Year's Day – what a fantastic way to start a new year!

Salmon Florentine

Serves 2
Preheat oven to 200C (400F)

225g / 8oz baby spinach leaves
10 small button mushrooms, sliced
1 clove garlic, minced
2 tsps olive oil
2 tsps lemon juice, freshly squeezed
2 tbsps butter
Salt and pepper to taste
2 salmon fillets, 170g / 6oz per serving, boned and skinned
1 tbsp flour
2 egg yolks
115g / 4oz chilled butter, cut into pieces
2 tsps cold water
1 tsp lemon juice
Pinch of dry mustard
Lemon wedges to garnish

Method:

1. Melt 1 tbsp of butter in a sauté pan, then sauté the mushrooms until they are just cooked. Add the lemon juice and a dash of salt and pepper. Set aside.
2. Heat the oil in a sauté pan, then add the minced garlic and sauté until fragrant. Add the spinach, and toss in the oil and garlic. Turn the heat to the lowest temperature and allow the spinach to wilt. Do not cover. Wilting will only take 1–2 minutes, so do not overcook. Add the mushrooms, toss to combine and set aside. Keep warm.
3. Dust the salmon in flour and shake off any excess (the flour

prevents the salmon from sticking to the pan.) Melt 1 tbsp of butter in a skillet and sear the salmon for 1–2 minutes per side. Transfer to a shallow ovenproof dish, and place in the oven for 6–10 minutes depending on the thickness of the fish. If in doubt, flake at a thick part of the fish with a fork to test. While fish is cooking, make the sauce.

4. Place the egg yolks in a shallow small saucepan over a low heat. Add the water and whisk constantly. Add the butter 1 piece at a time, whisking until each piece is thoroughly melted. Repeat until all the pieces are used. Add a pinch of dry mustard. Whisk in the lemon juice. If the sauce is thicker than desired, whisk in cold water a drop at a time until the right consistency is obtained. Keep the sauce warm over a pan of warm (not hot) water, or keep it warm in a flask.
5. To serve, place a bed of spinach onto a warmed plate, lay the salmon on the spinach, and drizzle with a small amount of sauce. Garnish with lemon wedges.

Serve with boiled baby potatoes.

Salmon with Pinot Noir Sauce

Serves 4
Preheat oven to 200C (400F)

Sauce

200ml / 8 fluid oz Pinot Noir wine
1 shallot, chopped
1 sprig thyme
2 juniper berries, squeezed between fingers to release aroma
100ml / 4 fluid oz chicken stock
50ml / 2 fluid oz cream
225g / 8oz butter cut into 1-inch pieces
¼ tsp coarsely cracked blacked pepper

Sauce method:

1. Pour the stock into a saucepan. Add the shallots, wine, thyme, juniper berries and pepper. Bring to boil over a medium heat and reduce for 10 minutes. Add the cream and reduce by half. Turn to the lowest setting and whisk in butter, one piece at a time, until all the butter has been incorporated.
2. Strain the sauce and keep it warm over a pan of warm water (not hot) or in a flask.

Salmon

4 salmon fillets (about 170g / 6oz each), boned and skinned.
2 tbsps flour
100ml / 4 fluid oz sunflower oil for cooking fish

Salmon method:

1. Dredge the salmon fillets in flour and shake to remove any excess flour. Heat the sunflower oil in a pan; sear the fillets for 1–2 minutes on each side until golden brown. Remove to a shallow ovenproof dish and bake for 6–10 minutes or until done. Test by flaking the fish with a fork.
2. Place a pool of sauce onto a warmed plate and position the salmon in the centre of the pool. Garnish with 4-inch lengths of chives.

Serve with Jansson's Temptation Potatoes (see page 99).

Sole with Sun-dried Tomato Buerre Blanc

Serves 2

Sauce

225g / 8oz butter, room temperature, cut into pieces
1 tbsp butter
1 tbsp cream
6 shallots, sliced
1 tbsp white wine vinegar
2 tbsps sun-dried tomatoes, chopped fine

Sauce method:

Sauté the shallots in 1 tbsp of butter until soft. Add the white wine vinegar and reduce by half. Add the cream and reduce slightly. Strain. The sauce can be made to this point and set aside to be reheated. To complete, reduce the heat to low and whisk in 225g / 8oz of butter a piece at a time, taking care that the sauce does not split. Add the sun-dried tomatoes, and keep the sauce warm in a flask until ready to serve.

Spinach

285g / 10oz fresh spinach
¼ tsp oregano
1 shallot, minced
¼ tsp ground nutmeg
2 tsps lemon juice, freshly squeezed
2 tsps toasted pine nuts
2 tsps olive oil

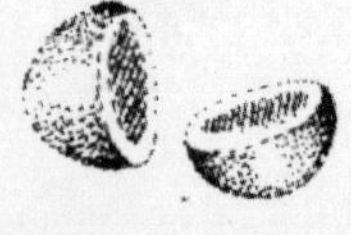

Spinach method:

Heat 2 tsps olive oil in a sauté pan, then add the shallots and cook until they are soft. Stir in the spinach; add the oregano and nutmeg. Salt to taste. Cook until heated through, then stir in the pine nuts and lemon juice. Cook for 2 minutes to allow the flavours to marry.

Sole

4 fillets of lemon sole (allow 170g / 6oz per serving)
1 tbsp flour
Sunflower oil

Sole method:

Dredge the sole in flour, then fry quickly in sunflower oil until the fish begins to brown around the edges (about 3 minutes). Turn the fish over and fry it on the other side for 1 minute. Transfer to a warmed plate.

Place a serving of spinach on a warmed plate. Place the fish on top and drizzle with sauce. Garnish with lemon wedges.

Serve with orzo.

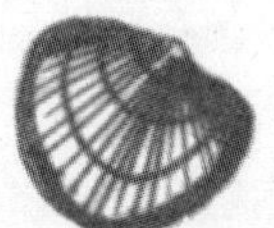
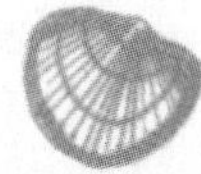
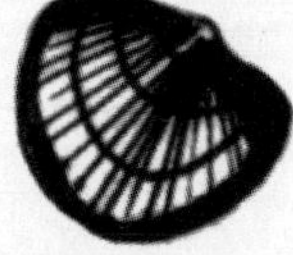

Baking & Sweets

Cheddar Pepper Bread

Makes 2 loaves
Preheat oven to 200C (400F)

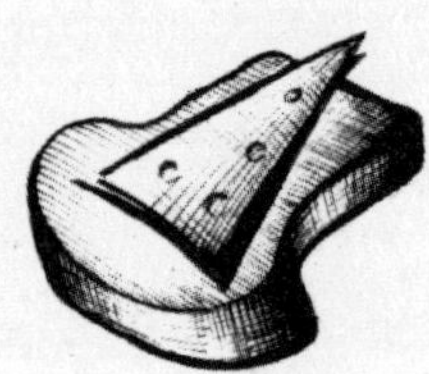

1 package active dry yeast
2 tsps salt
50ml / 2 fluid oz lukewarm water
225g / 8oz sharp cheddar cheese
2 tsps coarsely cracked black pepper
700g / 25oz strong white flour

Method:

1. Oil two 9x5-inch bread pans. Mix the yeast and 50ml / 2 fluid oz of lukewarm water in a small mixing bowl. Let it stand for 15 minutes.
2. Combine the flour and salt in a large mixing bowl. Make a well in the centre and pour in the yeast mixture. Add the remaining water and begin mixing the flour. Once combined place onto a floured surface and knead the dough for 10 minutes. It may be necessary to use additional flour if the dough is sticky. Place into a large oiled bowl, cover with a clean towel and place in a warm draught-free place for 1½ hours, or until it has doubled in size.
3. Punch down dough and then let it rest for 10 minutes. Place onto a floured surface, and flatten it into a large rectangular shape. Sprinkle with the cheese and pepper. Fold over the dough and begin kneading until it is smooth. Divide and shape it into 2 loaves before placing them in prepared pans. Let it rise in a draught-free place for 30 minutes, or until it has doubled in size.
4. Bake in a preheated oven for 30 minutes or until it is golden brown and sounds hollow when tapped on the bottom.

Date Muffins

Makes 36 muffins
Preheat oven to 190C (375F)

170g / 6oz chopped dates
1 tbsp bread soda
200ml / 8 fluid oz boiling water
225g / 8oz caster sugar
115g / 4oz butter
2 eggs
340g / 12oz strong white flour
115g / 4oz finely grated carrot
85g / 3oz currants
½ tsp salt
115g / 4oz All-Bran cereal
115g / 4oz chopped walnuts
400ml / 16 fluid oz buttermilk

Method:

1. Combine the dates, soda, and 200ml / 8 fluid oz of hot water. Stir and leave the mixture to cool at room temperature. Cream in the butter and sugar, then mix in the date mixture. Add the eggs one at a time, thoroughly mixing in each egg before adding the next. Gradually beat in the flour and salt.
2. Combine the cereal, walnuts, carrots, currants and buttermilk. Add to the flour mixture to complete batter.
3. Spoon into muffin tins lined with muffin papers. Fill ¾ full and bake at 190C (375F) for 20 minutes, or until it tests done when a skewer inserted into it comes out clean.

Hazelnut Wholewheat Bread

Makes 2 loaves
Preheat oven to 200C (400F)

455g / 16oz strong white flour
455g / 16oz coarse wholewheat flour
340g / 12oz wholewheat flour, fine ground
115g / 4oz hazelnuts, toasted, chopped fine
50ml / 2 fluid oz honey
28g / 1oz soft butter
1 tbsp dried yeast
2 tsps salt
400ml / 16 fluid oz lukewarm water

Method:

1. Combine the strong white flour and coarse wholewheat flour in a large bowl. Stir in the hazelnuts, yeast, salt, butter, and honey. Gradually add 100ml / 4 fluid oz of warm water, stirring all the time to mix the ingredients.
2. Stir in 170g / 6oz of the finely ground wholewheat flour; add enough of the remaining water to make a smooth non-sticky dough. (Add the remaining flour if needed.)
3. Knead the dough for 10 minutes. Place into an oiled large bowl, cover with a clean towel and let rise for 1½ hours in a warm draft-free place.
4. Punch the dough down, and then let it rest for 10 minutes. Oil 2 9x5x3-inch bread tins. Knead the dough to release any trapped air. Shape it into 2 loaves, then put into the oiled bread tins, and let them rise for 30 minutes in a draft-free place.
5. Bake at 200C (400F) in a preheated oven for 25–30 minutes.

The bread will sound hollow when it is tapped on the bottom. Cool in a pan for 10 minutes, then remove to a wire rack and cool completely.

An Bohreen Scones with Orange Butter

Makes 8–12 scones
Preheat oven to 200C (400F)

455g / 16oz strong white flour
2½ tbsps caster sugar
4½ tsps baking powder
¾ tsp salt
½ tsp cream of tartar
170g / 6oz butter, cut into pieces
150ml / 6 fluid oz milk
1 egg, beaten

Method:

1. Sieve the flour, sugar, baking powder, salt and crème of tartar in a food processor. With the motor running, add the butter a piece at a time through the feed tube. Process until the mixture resembles a coarse meal.
2. Mix the egg and milk in jug.
3. Pour the flour mixture into a large bowl. Make a well in the centre and add the milk and egg mixture. Stir well to combine and turn it out onto a floured work surface. Knead 2–3 times to tidy the dough, then roll it out or pat it down until it is 1-inch thick. Do not over-work the dough or the scones will not be tender. The key is to handle the dough mixture as little as possible.
4. Cut out the scones and place them onto a baking sheet, allowing plenty of room for expansion.
5. Bake for 15–20 minutes or until golden brown.

Orange butter

225g / 8oz butter, soft
200g / 7oz icing sugar
4 tsps orange zest

Orange Butter method:

Combine all of the ingredients in a mixing bowl and beat with an electric mixer until light and fluffy. Let the mixture sit in a refrigerator overnight to allow the flavour to develop.

Serve at room temperature on scones.

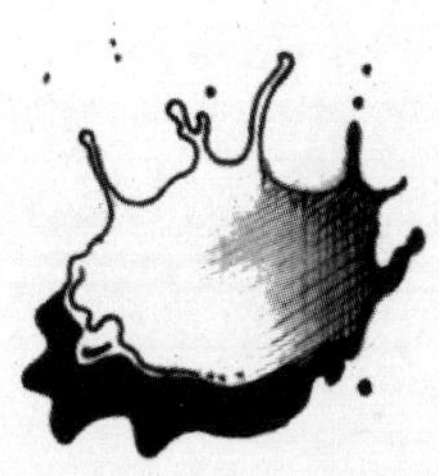

Naan Bread

Makes 10 pieces
Preheat oven to 180C (350F)

455g / 16oz strong white flour
1 tbsp plain yogurt
1 tsp baking powder
1 egg
400ml / 16 fluid oz water
1 tsp salt
1 tsp caster sugar

Method:

1. Mix all of the dry ingredients in a bowl, then make a well in centre.
2. Combine the egg and yogurt and pour into the well. Add the water slowly, stirring all the time to form a soft dough. The mixture should leave the sides of the bowl. Knead the dough until it becomes elastic, then pinch off 10 pieces. Let the pieces rest on a pan, covered with a damp towel for 1 hour.
3. Pat the dough into thin discs about 6 inches wide. Place onto a baking sheet and bake at 180C (350F) until it is puffy and begins to brown.

Rosemary Walnut Bread

Makes 2 loaves
Preheat oven to 190C (380F)

Combine in a small bowl:

400ml / 16 fluid oz warm milk
50ml / 2 fluid oz lukewarm water
2 tbsps honey
2 tbsps butter, melted
2 tsps salt

Add:

4½ tsps dried yeast
310g / 11oz strong white flour

Let it sit for 15 minutes, then add:

365g / 13oz strong white flour
115g / 4oz chopped walnuts
3 tbsps coarsely chopped fresh rosemary
1 egg, beaten

Method:

1. Stir the ingredients well to combine. Knead for 10 minutes, adding up to 115g / 4oz of flour, if needed, to create a non-sticky dough. Let the dough rise, covered and in a large oiled bowl in a draught-free place for 1 hour, or until it has doubled in volume.
2. Punch the dough down, then let it rest for 10 minutes. Knead and shape it into 2 loaves. Place the loaf mixtures into 2 oiled bread tins and let them rise for 30 minutes. Cut a slash down the centre of each and brush with 2 tbsps cream.
3. Bake at 190C (380F) for 30–40 minutes or until the bread

sounds hollow when it is tapped on the bottom. If the bread begins to brown too quickly, cover it loosely with kitchen foil.

4. Remove the bread from the oven, and allow it to cool in the pan for 10 minutes before moving it to a wire rack to cool completely.

Sun-dried Tomato Bread

Makes 2 loaves
Preheat oven to 200C (400F)

500ml / 20 fluid oz lukewarm water
4 tsps dried yeast
1 tsp honey
365g / 13oz strong white flour
280g / 10oz wholewheat flour
2 tsps salt
140g / 5oz drained and chopped oil-packed sun-dried tomatoes; reserve the oil
55g / 2oz freshly grated Parmesan cheese

Method:

1. Put 100ml / 4 fluid oz of water in a small bowl, add the yeast and honey and let it sit for 10 minutes.
2. Combine the flours, salt, sun-dried tomatoes and cheese. Add the yeast mixture and the remaining water. Stir well to combine.
3. Turn the dough out onto a floured surface and knead for 10 minutes.
4. Place the dough into an oiled bowl, cover with a clean towel, and place into a draught-free place to rise for 1 hour or until it has doubled in volume.
5. Punch the dough down and let it rest for 10 minutes. Knead and shape it into 2 loaves, then place them into oiled bread tins (use reserved sun-dried tomato oil) and let them rise in a draught-free location for 30 minutes. Bake at 200C (400F) for 30 minutes.

Wholewheat Honey Bread

Makes 4 loaves
Preheat oven to 200C (400F)

400ml / 16 fluid oz heated (not boiled) milk
2 tbsps butter
1 tbsp salt
800g / 28oz strong white flour
800g / 28oz wholewheat flour

Method:

1. Combine in measuring jug, add 200ml / 8 fluid oz of honey.
2. Dissolve 2 packages dried yeast in 200ml / 8 fluid oz lukewarm water. Let proof for 10 minutes.
3. Combine 680g / 24oz strong white flour and 680g / 24oz wholewheat flour.
4. Add half of the flour to the yeast mixture. Gradually add the milk mixture and the remainder of the flour. The dough should be somewhat stiff. If necessary add 85g / 3oz white flour.
5. Knead for 10 minutes. Place into a large oiled bowl, cover with a clean towel and let it rise in a warm draught-free place for 1 hour or until it has doubled in volume. Punch it down and let it rest for 10 minutes.
6. Knead the dough into 4 smooth loaves, and place into oiled bread tins. Let them rise for 30 minutes or until they have doubled in size.
7. Bake the loaves at 200C (400F) for 30 minutes, or until they sound hollow when tapped on the bottom.
8. Remove the loaves to a wire rack and allow to cool.

Almond Pastry Crust

Makes 1 crust
Preheat oven to 180C (350F)

225g / 8oz strong white flour
225g / 8oz ground blanched almonds
¼ tsp salt
1 tbsp caster sugar
115g / 4oz butter, chilled
3–4 tbsps cold water
1 drop almond essence

Method:

1. Combine the flour, almonds, salt, sugar, and almond essence. Cut in the butter and add cold water, one tbsp at a time.
2. Shape into a flattened disc, then wrap in cling film and chill for 30 minutes.
3. Roll out the dough placed between 2 sheets of cling film and fit it into a 10-inch tart pan.
4. Line the pastry with baking parchment, fill with beans or rice and blind bake for 15 minutes at 180C (350F). Remove from the oven. Remove the paper and beans or rice and cool for 10 minutes. Fill the dough and bake at 180C (350F) until the filling is done.

This is an excellent pastry for lemon, lime or almond tarts.

Shortcrust Pastry

Makes 2 pie crusts

365g / 13oz strong white flour
1 tsp salt
1 tsp sugar
225g / 8oz butter
50ml / 2 fluid oz ice-cold water

Method:

1. Combine the flour, salt, and sugar in a large mixing bowl.
2. Cut the butter into 1-inch cubes. With a pastry cutter or a knife cut butter cubes into flour. When the mixture resembles coarse meal, add cold water. Work into a ball, divide in half, and flatten into 2 discs. Wrap in cling film and chill for 30 minutes before using.
3. Bring it to room temperature and roll it out between 2 sheets of cling film. Line a pastry pan and proceed with recipe for any filled pie, quiche or tart.

Macadamia & Crumb Crust

Makes 1 tart crust
Preheat oven to 190C (375F)

Crust

115g / 4oz macadamia nuts
200g / 7oz digestive biscuit crumbs
(or graham crackers)
3 tbsps caster sugar
55g / 2oz butter, melted

Method:

In a food processor, chop the nuts into small pieces with on/off pulses. Add the digestive biscuits and sugar, and process them to combine. Add the butter and continue processing. Press into a 9-inch pan and bake until it is golden brown – this should take about 12 minutes.

Cool completely before filling with sour cream lemon pie.

Chocolate Almond Cake

Serves 12–16
Preheat oven to 180C (350F)

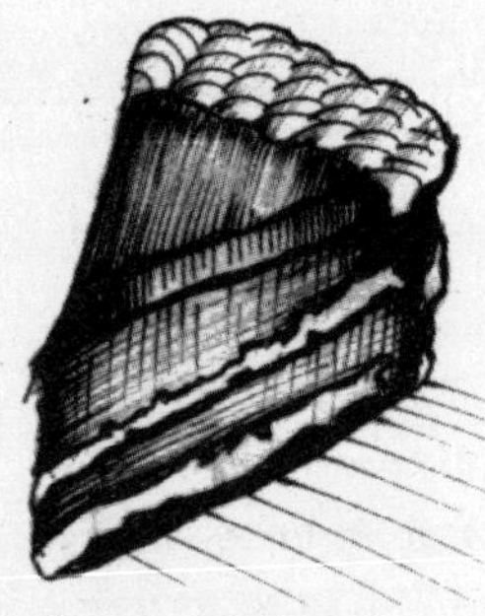

9 eggs, separated, room temperature
170g / 6oz caster sugar
2 tsps pure vanilla extract
Pinch of salt
¼ tsp cream of tartar
85g / 3oz unsweetened cocoa powder
400g / 14oz almond paste, no substitutions
2 tbsps brandy
Icing sugar
150ml / 6 fluid oz amaretto liqueur
455g / 16oz jar raspberry jam

Chocolate filling

200g / 7oz dark semi-sweet chocolate (70% cocoa)
3 tbsps butter
300ml / 12 fluid oz cream, room temperature
400ml / 16 fluid oz whipped cream for decorating

Cake method:

1. Line a 10x15x1-inch jelly roll pan with baking parchment, cut to fit the bottom of the pan. Butter the parchment and set the pan aside.
2. Beat the egg yolks, caster sugar, vanilla and salt in a mixer until the mix is pale yellow and ribbons form when the beaters are lifted from the bowl. Beat the whites with the cream

of tartar in a clean bowl until peaks form. Fold in part of the whites into the yolks to lighten the batter, and then add the rest of the whites. Sift in the cocoa, and gently fold to combine. Spread into a prepared pan, bake for 25 minutes or until it springs back when pressed on.

3. Blend the almond paste with 1 tbsp brandy. Knead until it is soft; then roll it out between 2 sheets of parchment paper into a 9x14-inch rectangle.
4. Dust a tea towel with some icing sugar. Turn the cake out onto the towel, then trim the edges of the cake. Place the almond paste onto the cake while it is still warm. Roll up the cake, starting on the long side. Leave in the towel and allow to cool.
5. Line a 10-inch spring form pan with some aluminium foil. Pour the amaretto into a dish. Cut the cake into one-third-inch slices; then dip one side briefly into the amaretto. Cover the bottom of the pan with dipped side down. Next cover the sides, press the slices firmly to adhere to the sides of the pan. Do not worry about the edges that rise above the top of the pan – these will be trimmed away later. Refrigerate.

Filling method:

Melt the chocolate and butter in a glass bowl over a pan of simmering water. Do not let the bottom of the bowl touch the water. Stir until the mixture is velvety and smooth. Add the cream slowly, folding until it is just combined. Spread a thin layer of raspberry jam over the cake layer on the bottom of the pan. Pour the chocolate mixture into the pan. Cover and refrigerate overnight.

To serve:

Trim the edges of the cake to make cake even with filling. Invert onto serving plate. Leave for ½ hour and then decorate the edges with whipped cream to create a finished appearance.

Christmas Cake

Makes 2 cakes

Preheat oven to 150C (300F). Butter 2 9-inch round, 3-inch deep pans. Line with aluminium foil and butter foil.

1) Sift into a large bowl:

340g / 12oz strong white flour
430g / 15oz caster sugar
1 tsp baking powder
1 tsp salt

2) Add to flour mixture:

430g / 15oz raisins
455g / 16oz candied peel
900g / 32oz red maraschino cherries, drained
500g / 18oz pecan halves
(mix well to coat in flour mixture)

Cake method

1. Beat 6 eggs until they become thick and light coloured, then add 50ml / 2 fluid oz of dark rum and an equal amount of brandy. Pour this over the fruit mixture and stir well. Fill the pans and press the batter into the pan.
2. Bake at 150C (300F) for 1½ hours or until a wooden skewer comes out clean when inserted in the centre. Allow to cool in a pan on a rack for 30 minutes, then remove it from the pan and let it cool completely.
3. When the cake is completely cool, wrap it in muslin that has been dampened in brandy. Wrap it tightly in foil and store in a cake tin with a tight-fitting lid for at least 2 months.
4. Brush the cake with apricot jam, then cover with marzipan and royal or fondant icing.

Marzipan method:

Use approximately 455g / 16oz prepared marzipan. Roll the marzipan out onto a flat surface that has been dusted with icing sugar. Roll out a slightly larger area than the top of the cake. Lay the marzipan onto the cake top. Trim the edges. Measure around the sides of the cake with a piece of kitchen twine. Roll out a strip of marzipan of the right height and length to cover the sides. Roll up the strip loosely, and then unroll it against the sides of the cake. Using a palette knife smooth the edge of the cake where the sides and top join. Allow to set for 2 days to dry.

Fondant:

Makes about 900g / 32oz

780g / 28oz icing sugar
2 fresh egg whites
100ml / 4 fluid oz liquid glucose

Fondant method:

1. Sift the sugar into a bowl. Make a well in the centre, then add the egg white and glucose. Beat well with a spoon. When the mixture becomes stiff turn it out onto a surface dusted with icing sugar. Knead until it is smooth. Wrap it in cling film until it is ready to use.
2. To cover the marzipan-coated cake, roll the icing out on to a surface sprinkled with corn flour. Roll it out so it is 6 inches larger than the cake.
3. Drape it onto the rolling pin and place it on the cake. Dust your hands with corn flour and press the icing against the cake. Trim any excess from the bottom of the cake.
4. Allow to dry for 2 days. Decorate in your chosen manner or use the excess fondant to form leaves, flowers, or balls. Stick these to the decorated cake with some beaten egg white.

Harvest Apple Cake

Makes 1 cake
Preheat oven to 170C (325F)

285g / 10oz unpeeled Granny Smith apples, cored and diced
285g / 10oz unpeeled Cox or Braeburn apples, cored and diced
455g / 16oz caster sugar
430g / 15oz flour
2 tsps bread soda
1 tsp salt
2 tsps ground cinnamon
1 tsp ground allspice
½ tsp nutmeg
½ tsp mace
200ml / 8 fluid oz sunflower oil
2 large eggs, beaten
50ml / 2 fluid oz brandy
225g / 8oz walnuts, chopped coarsely
115g / 4oz golden sultanas
115g / 4oz raisins
55g / 2oz currants

Decoration:

1 Braeburn or Cox apple
55g / 2oz chopped walnuts
55g / 2oz apricot jam, warmed and strained

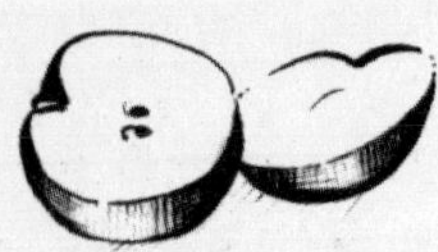

Method:

1. Butter and dust with flour a 9-inch spring form pan, and line the base with some parchment. Set aside.
2. Combine the apples and sugar in a large bowl and let sit for 20 minutes.
3. Combine the flour, soda, salt and spices in a large bowl. Add the oil, eggs, brandy and apples. Stir to combine but do not over-mix. Fold in the nuts, raisins, sultanas, and currants. Pour into a prepared pan, and level the mix with a palette knife.
4. Decorate the top of the cake with some thinly sliced apples and chopped nuts. Bake for 1¼ hours or until a tester comes out clean when inserted in the centre. Cool in a pan for 10 minutes, then move it to a wire rack.

Brush with some jam while it is still warm and serve.

Irish Cream with Raspberry Sauce

Serves 6

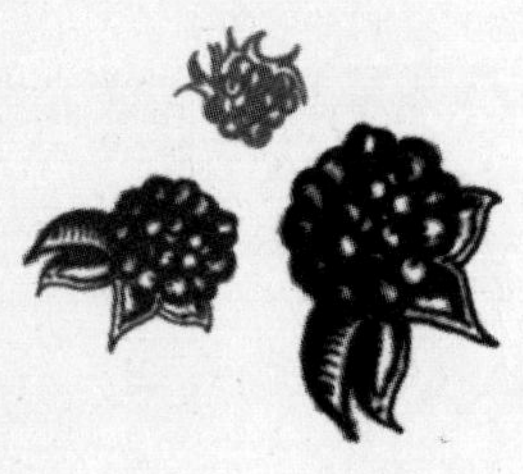

2 tsps unflavoured gelatine powder
1 tbsp cold water
400ml / 16 fluid oz cream
115g / 4oz caster sugar
125ml / 5 fluid oz sour cream
50ml / 2 fluid oz plain yogurt
½ tsp pure vanilla extract
2 tbsps Irish whiskey

Method:

1. Soften 2 tsps of gelatine in 1 tbsp of cold water in a small saucepan.
2. Add the cream and caster sugar to the saucepan. Place over a medium heat and stir until the gelatine is completely dissolved. Do not allow it to boil. Remove it from the heat and allow to cool.
3. Fold in the sour cream, yogurt, vanilla and whiskey. Whisk to combine.
4. Pour the mixture into 6 decorative glasses or wine glasses. Cover with some cling film and refrigerate for at least 3 hours, preferably overnight.
5. Top with 2–3 tbsps of the fruit sauce and a dollop of whipped cream.

Raspberry Sauce

285g / 10oz frozen raspberries
115g / 4oz currant jam
115g / 4oz caster sugar

1 tsp corn flour
75ml / 3 fluid oz cassis
½ tsp fresh lemon juice

Raspberry Sauce method:

1. Combine the berries, sugar and currant jam in a saucepan, then stir over a moderate heat until the mixture comes to a boil. Add 1 tsp corn flour dissolved in 1 tsp cold water. Simmer for 10 minutes.
2. Add the cassis and ½ tsp lemon juice. Strain and chill.
3. The sauce can be made ahead and frozen until needed. Simply set into a pan of room temperature water to thaw.

Garnish with a mint leaf.

Luscious Sour Cream Lemon Pie

Makes 1 pie

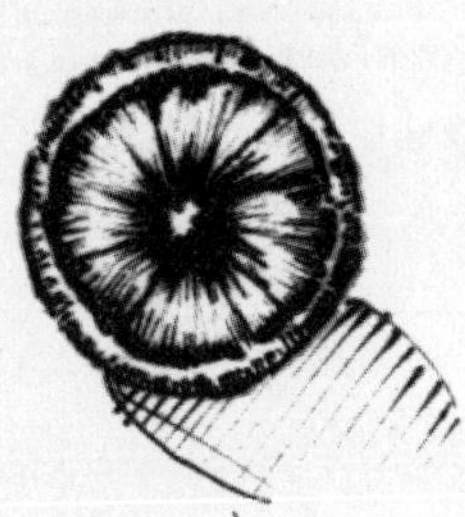

1 9-inch baked short crust or macadamia crumb crust
55g / 2oz caster sugar
55g / 2oz corn flour
2 eggs
100ml / 4 fluid oz fresh lemon juice
50ml / 2 fluid oz lemoncello liqueur
50ml / 2 fluid oz boiling water
1 tbsp butter
Few drops of yellow food colouring
100ml / 4 fluid oz sour cream, room temperature

Method:

1. In a saucepan, combine the sugar, corn flour and eggs. Whisk together to combine over a medium heat and gradually stir in the lemon juice, lemoncello and water. Stir constantly, and cook until the mixture comes to a boil and thickens. Cook for 1 minute more, whisking all the time.
2. Remove from the heat, then whisk in the butter. Add some food colouring if desired. Fold in the sour cream and pour into the crust. Chill.

Garnish with whipped cream and twists of lemon peel.

My Mother's Fresh Coconut Cake

Makes 1 cake

Preheat oven to 170C (325F)

Batter

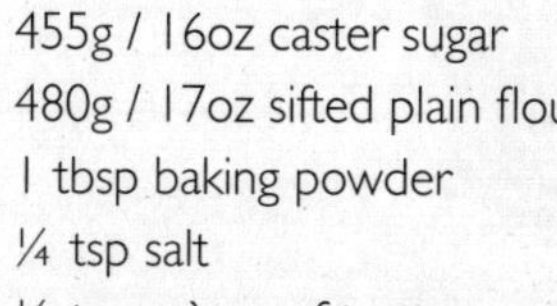

225g / 8oz butter, softened

455g / 16oz caster sugar

480g / 17oz sifted plain flour

1 tbsp baking powder

¼ tsp salt

¼ tsp crème of tartar

1 tsp pure vanilla extract

200ml / 8 fluid oz milk

8 large egg whites

Method:

1. Butter and flour three 9-inch round cake tins. Line the bottoms with parchment. Beat the butter and sugar until they become light and fluffy.
2. Combine the dry ingredients and sift them into a bowl. Fold the dry ingredients into the butter mixture alternately with milk, beginning and ending with flour.
3. In a clean bowl beat the egg whites until they are stiff but not dry. Fold one-third of the egg whites into the batter to lighten it, and then fold in the rest of the egg whites. Use care when folding to prevent deflating egg whites. Use a large rubber spatula to accomplish this.
4. Spoon into the prepared cake tins and bake for 25 minutes or until a tester comes out clean when inserted in the centre. Cool for 10 minutes in the pan, then move them carefully to wire racks to cool further.

American Seven-Minute Frosting

Preheat oven to 180C (375F)

2 large egg whites
340g / 12oz caster sugar
2 tsps golden syrup
¼ tsp cream of tartar
½ tsp pure vanilla extract
Cold water

Method:

Combine the egg whites, sugar, golden syrup, and cream of tartar with 5 tbsps of cold water in the top of a double-boiler. As the water in the base boils, beat the mixture with a hand mixer for 4 minutes at a low speed, then beat for 4 minutes on a high speed. Turn off the heat, add the vanilla, and continue beating until the frosting holds stiff peaks (this should take 2–5 minutes). Take care not to over-beat, as the frosting will become grainy. The frosting should be fluffy and shiny.

Coconuts

2 coconuts

Coconut method:

1. Pierce the eyes at the ends of the coconut with a skewer and a hammer, then drain the liquid into a measuring jug. Use this liquid to brush the tops of the cake before frosting. Taste the liquid to ensure it is not spoiled – it should taste faintly sweet.
2. Place the drained coconuts into a preheated 180C (375F) oven for 20 minutes. When they are cool tap them with a

hammer; this will help to release the meat from the shell. Cover the coconuts with a towel and then break them open with the hammer. Peel the rough skin from the coconut with a vegetable peeler or paring knife. Grate the coconut with a food grater.

To assemble:

Brush the cake layers with the coconut liquid. Place one layer on a serving plate, then cover the top with some frosting, and dust with grated coconut. Repeat with the next layer. Top with a third layer, then cover the top and sides with more frosting. With a palette knife, decorate the top of the cake with peaks of frosting. Dust the top and sides with more grated coconut.

Once frosted do not store the cake in a refrigerator or in plastic. The cake will keep at room temperature for a few days.

New York Cheesecake

Makes 1 cake
Preheat oven to 170C (325F)

1 tbsp room temperature butter
170g / 6oz digestive biscuits ground
1200g / 48oz cream cheese, room temperature
620g / 22oz caster sugar
155g / 5½oz corn flour
¼ tsp salt
6 eggs, large
6 egg yolks, large
100ml / 4 fluid oz cream
50ml / 2 fluid oz milk
Grated peel of 1 lemon
Juice of 1 lemon
½ tsp pure vanilla extract

Method:

1. Butter the sides and bottom of a 10-inch spring form pan. Dust the bottom and sides with ground digestive biscuits. Pat the remaining crumbs onto the bottom of the pan.
2. Beat the cream cheese in a large mixing bowl until it becomes soft and fluffy.
3. Combine the sugar, corn flour and salt, and whisk to thoroughly mix. Blend this into the cream cheese. Add the eggs and egg yolks, alternately, beating well with each addition. Stir with a rubber spatula to ensure there are no lumps.
4. Stir in the milk, cream, grated peel, juice and vanilla. Pour into the prepared pan.
5. Place a large baking pan or broiler pan full of water on the lowest rack of the oven (this prevents cheesecake from

cracking during baking). Place the spring form pan in the middle of the oven. Bake for 1 hour 40 minutes or until the centre is solid. Turn off the heat, do not open the oven door, and leave to sit for 2 hours. Remove and refrigerate. It is preferable to make this one day before to give it time to chill properly.

Garnish with fruit, coulis or whipped cream.

Oatmeal Fudge Cake

Makes 24 squares
Preheat oven to 180C (350F)

365g / 13oz oatmeal, cooked
140g / 5oz strong white flour
340g / 12oz caster sugar
115g / 2oz unsweetened cocoa powder
1 tsp baking soda
½ tsp salt
115g / 4oz butter, melted and cooled
1 tsp pure vanilla extract
1 tbsp instant espresso powder, dissolved in 1 tbsp hot water
2 eggs
115g / 2oz finely chopped walnuts
Icing sugar (optional)

Method:

1. In large mixing bowl, stir together the flour, sugar, cocoa, salt and soda. Add the butter, cooked oatmeal, vanilla and espresso; beat at a low speed until mixed, then at medium speed for 2 more minutes. Add the eggs and beat for a further 2 minutes at medium speed. Fold in the walnuts.
2. Pour into a 13x9x2-inch buttered pan.
3. Bake for 35 minutes or until a cocktail stick comes out clean when inserted in the centre. Cool in the pan for 10 minutes, then remove it from the pan and allow it to cool on a wire rack. The cake will fall slightly.
4. Dust the top with icing sugar if desired, then cut into 24 squares.

Store for a day or two and the cake will improve.

Oatmeal Raisin Cookies

Makes 25 cookies
Preheat oven to 180C (350F)

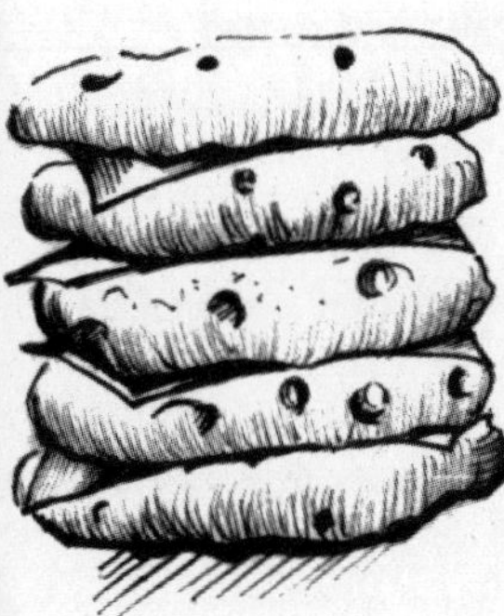

170g / 6oz butter
115g / 4oz granulated sugar
225g / 8oz soft brown sugar
1 egg
25ml / 1 fluid oz water
1 tsp pure vanilla extract
100g / 3½oz flour
1 tsp cinnamon
½ tsp salt
255g / 9oz porridge oats
140g / 5oz raisins
140g / 5oz chopped walnuts

Method:

1. Cream the butter and sugars together until they are fluffy, then add the egg, beat well and add the water and vanilla.
2. Sift together the dry ingredients, then add this to the sugar mixture and mix it well. Fold in the oats, raisins and walnuts.
3. Shape into balls, then place them onto a baking sheet and bake for 15–17 minutes or until the edges are done and the centres are still a bit soft. Cool on a wire rack.

If a crisper cookie is desired, simply bake them for longer.

Pecan Pie

Serves 8–10
Preheat oven to 180C (350F)

250ml / 10 fluid oz golden syrup or corn syrup
225g / 8oz soft brown sugar
6 eggs
55g / 2oz butter, melted and cooled
1 tsp pure vanilla extract
25ml / 1 fluid oz bourbon
225g / 8oz coarsely chopped pecans
115g / 4oz pecan halves, used for decorating top
1 9-inch unbaked short crust pastry

Method:

1. Line a 9-inch pie dish with pastry, then set it aside.
2. Pour the golden syrup and brown sugar into a medium saucepan. Bring to the boil, then remove from the heat, and add the chopped pecans, 55g / 2oz of melted butter, beaten eggs, bourbon, and vanilla. Stir to combine, then pour the mix into the pastry crust. Decorate the top with the pecan halves.
3. Bake for 45–50 minutes, or until the filling is set when the pan is jiggled. If the top of the pie begins to brown too quickly, tent aluminium foil loosely over it.

Cool completely, then garnish with whipped cream. If this is not rich enough, sprinkle with some chocolate pieces.

Rich Chocolate Mousse

170g / 6oz (70% cocoa) chocolate
100ml / 4 fluid oz heated crème de cacao
115g / 4oz butter, room temperature, cut into pieces
4 eggs, separated
2 tbsps icing sugar

Method:

1. Combine the chocolate, broken into pieces, warmed crème de cacao, butter and egg yolks in a blender. Blend until the mixture is smooth, then pour it into a large bowl.
2. Beat 4 egg whites until they are stiff, then fold in 2 tbsps of icing sugar. Gently fold the egg whites into the chocolate mixture. Using a large rubber spatula stir in a circular motion and mix thoroughly.
3. Pour 55g / 2oz of the mousse into small dishes or decorative glasses. Let them chill for several hours or overnight.

Garnish with raspberry puree, fruit coulis, whipped cream, or grated chocolate.

Summer Berry Patch Pie

Makes 1 pie
Preheat oven to 180C (350F)

Crust

455g / 16oz strong white flour
½ tsp salt
200g / 7oz butter, chilled
and cut into pieces
1–2 tbsps cold water
Egg yolk and 2 tsps water
– whisk together for glaze

Filling

225g / 8oz blackberries
225g / 8oz raspberries
225g / 8oz strawberries
225g / 8oz rhubarb, chopped
455g / 16oz Granny Smith apples,
peeled, cored, and chopped
225g / 8oz caster sugar
55g / 2oz flour
1 tbsp fresh lemon juice
Pinch of nutmeg

Method:

1. Sift the flour into a bowl, and add salt. Mix in the butter until the mixture resembles a coarse meal. Add the cold water little by little until the mixture holds together. Divide it in half, then shape into a flattened disc and wrap it in cling film. Chill the pastry for 30 minutes.
2. Roll the pastry out between 2 sheets of cling film. Fit into a deep 9-inch pie dish and fill it with the mixture.

3. Combine the apples, rhubarb, flour and sugar, then toss in the berries and fill the pie crust. Roll out the top crust. Brush the bottom crust edges with water and fit on top crust. Crimp the edges.
4. Brush the top pastry with egg yolk/water mixture and cut slits in it to let steam escape.
5. Bake at 180C (350F) for 50–60 minutes or until it is golden brown.

Place a liner under pie as juice can drip and this will save a messy clean up later. Garnish with whipped cream or luscious vanilla ice cream.

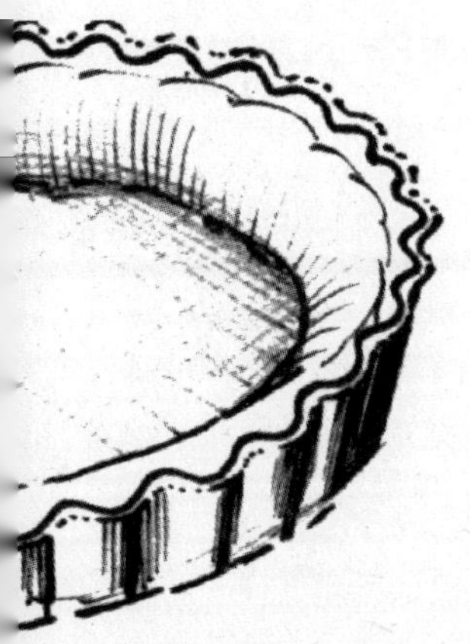

White Chocolate Pecan Bread Pudding

Serves 6
Preheat oven to 150C (300F)

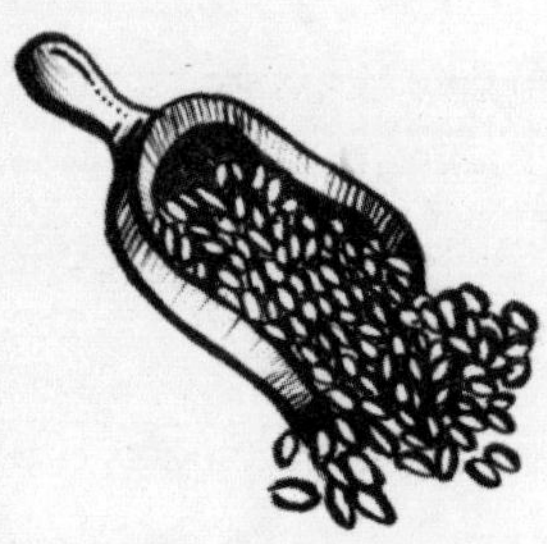

1 package croissants or a loaf of brioche
250ml / 10 fluid oz milk
200ml / 8 fluid oz cream
8 eggs
225g / 8oz caster sugar
1 tsp pure vanilla extract
1 tsp cinnamon
170g / 6oz white chocolate pieces
170g / 6oz pecans, chopped

Method:

1. Butter and line with parchment a 9x5x3-inch loaf pan.
2. Cube the bread and place it into the prepared pan, then add the nuts and chocolate pieces.
3. Combine together the milk, cream, eggs, sugar, vanilla, cinnamon, and pour this mixture over the bread. Push it down with your fingers to release air. Let it stand for 60 minutes or longer to absorb the liquid.
4. Cover with parchment and foil, then bake in a *bain marie* or larger roasting pan with water half way up the sides, for 1 to 1½ hours. During the last 15 minutes, remove the top covering to allow the top to brown. Test with a skewer to check that the pudding is cooked.

Serve with crème anglaise.

Crème Anglaise

200ml / 8 fluid oz cream
115g / 4oz caster sugar
Vanilla bean, split and seeds loosened
with the point of a knife
4 egg yolks
2 tbsps butter

Method:

1. Place the egg yolks in a bowl and whisk in 55g / 2oz sugar.
2. Combine the cream, rest of sugar and vanilla bean in a saucepan over a medium heat. When the cream comes to a boil, remove it from the heat and mix 50ml / 2 fluid oz of it into the egg yolks.
3. Add the rest of the egg yolks to the cream, whisking to combine.
4. Return to the heat and cook over medium until the mixture is thick enough to coat the back of a spoon. Stir in the butter and serve warm or at room temperature.

The mixture can only be warmed gently, preferably over warm water.

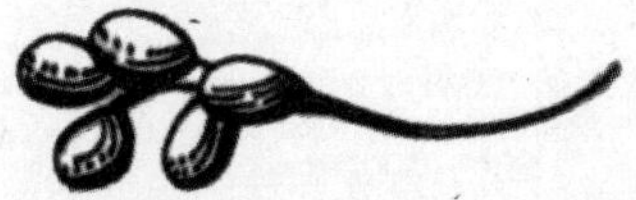

An Bohreen Brown Bread

Makes 1 loaf
Preheat oven to 200C (400F)

285g / 10oz coarse wholemeal flour
170g / 6oz strong white flour
2 heaped tbsps oat bran
1 tsp salt
½ tsp bread soda, sieve into flour
2 tsps soft brown sugar
375ml / 15 fluid oz buttermilk
1 egg
2 tbsps sunflower oil

Method:

1. Oil a 9x5x3-inch bread tin. Place all of the dry ingredients into a large bowl and make a well in the centre. Whisk together the buttermilk, sunflower oil, and egg. Pour the mixture into the well and mix thoroughly. The mixture should be wet and sloppy. Pour it immediately into a prepared bread tin. Cut a deep slit down the centre of the batter – this lets the evil fairies out.
2. Bake for approximately 60 minutes or until the bread sounds hollow when tapped on the bottom.
3. Cool on the wire rack. If a softer crust is desired wrap the bread in a clean kitchen towel when removed from the oven, then cool on a wire rack.

Jams

My Mother's Dried Apricot Pineapple Jam

Makes 1–1½ litres / 32–48 fluid oz

455g / 16oz dried apricots
455g / 16oz drained crushed pineapple
Juice of 1 lemon
900g / 32oz granulated sugar

Method:

1. Cover the apricots with cold water and let them soak overnight to plump and soften them.
2. The next day put the mixture into a large pot and simmer until the apricots are tender. Warm the sugar in the oven. Mash the apricots; add the pineapple, lemon juice and sugar. Simmer until the mixture is thick and the liquid is clear. Test by dropping a bit of jam onto a chilled saucer, pop it into the freezer for a minute, then remove it and push the jam with your finger. If it is set the jam will wrinkle when pushed. If not, cook gently for a few more minutes and re-test.
3. Pour the jam the into clean hot jars. Wipe the top of each jar with a clean wet cloth to remove any splatters. If you are using lids, place the lids in a saucepan with boiling water, boil for 1 minute and then place onto the jars. Tighten the lids and leave to rest. The jars should make a popping sound as they seal.

Store in a dark, cool place.

Peach Jam

Makes 2–3 litres / 64–96 fluid oz

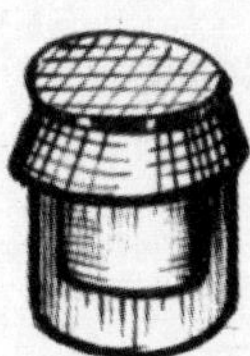

900g / 32oz peeled and crushed peaches
50ml / 2 fluid oz freshly squeezed lemon juice
675g / 24oz granulated sugar
1 cinnamon stick

Method:

1. Combine the peaches, cinnamon stick and lemon juice in a large pot. Cook over a medium heat for 15 minutes, then remove the cinnamon stick.
2. Add the sugar and stir to dissolve. Bring to a boil and cook for 15 minutes, stirring often to prevent scorching.
3. Test the jam by dropping a bit of jam onto a chilled saucer, popping it into a freezer for a minute, removing it and pushing the jam with your finger. If it is set, the jam will wrinkle when it is pushed. If not, cook it gently for a few more minutes and then re-test.
4. Pour the jam the into clean hot jars. Wipe the top of each jar with a clean wet cloth to remove any splatters. If you are using lids, place the lids in a saucepan with boiling water, boil for 1 minute and then place onto the jars. Tighten the lids and leave to rest. The jars should make a popping sound as they seal. Store in a dark, cool place.

Nectarines can be substituted for peaches.

Whiskey Seville Orange Marmalade

Makes 2–3 litres / 64–96 fluid oz

900g / 32oz Seville oranges
1600ml / 64 fluid oz water
1 lemon
1800g / 64oz granulated sugar
50ml / 2 fluid oz Irish whiskey

Method:

1. Wash the oranges and lemon to remove any wax. Cut in half and squeeze out the juice. Remove the pulp with a dessertspoon. Combine the pulp and pips in a muslin cloth and tie into a ball. Place the ball in a large bowl and cover with water. Let stand while cutting rinds.
2. Cut each rind in half, then place on a cutting board and slice thinly. Put into a bowl with the pulp ball, add the remainder of the water and soak overnight.
3. Pour the contents of the bowl into a large pan and bring to a boil. Simmer for 2 hours or until the peel is soft when squeezed gently between your fingers.
4. Squeeze the liquid from the muslin ball into a pot. While cooking, warm the sugar and jars in the oven. Add the warmed sugar to the pot and stir well to dissolve.
5. Bring the mixture to a boil, and cook until the marmalade is set. Add whiskey if desired.
6. Test the jam by dropping a bit of jam onto a chilled saucer, popping it into a freezer for a minute, removing it and pushing the jam with your finger. If it is set, the jam will wrinkle when it is pushed. If not, cook it gently for a few more minutes and then re-test.

7. Pour the jam the into clean hot jars. Wipe the top of each jar with a clean wet cloth to remove any splatters. If you are using lids, place the lids in a saucepan with boiling water, boil 1 minute then place onto the jars. Tighten the lids and leave to rest. The jars should make a popping sound as they seal. Store in a dark, cool place.

I included this because so many of our guests requested the recipe.
Enjoy.

Raspberry Jam

Makes 2–3 litres / 64–96 fluid oz

900g / 32oz raspberries
900g / 32oz sugar

Method:

1. Warm the sugar in the oven.
2. Put the berries into a large saucepan and cook until the juice begins to flow (this should take about 5–10 minutes). Add the warmed sugar and stir to dissolve it. Bring to a full boil and cook for 5–15 minutes.
3. Test the jam by dropping a bit of jam onto a chilled saucer, popping it into a freezer for a minute, removing it and pushing the jam with your finger. If it is set, the jam will wrinkle when it is pushed. If not, cook it gently for a few more minutes and then re-test. Pour the jam the into clean hot jars.
4. Wipe the top of each jar with a clean wet cloth to remove any splatters. If you are using lids, place them in a saucepan with boiling water, boil for 1 minute and then place onto the jars. Tighten the lids and leave to rest. The jars should make a popping sound as they seal.

Store in a dark, cool place.

Strawberry Rhubarb Jam

Makes 2–3 litres / 64–96 fluid oz

900g / 32oz strawberries
900g / 32oz rhubarb
1350g / 48oz granulated sugar

Method:

1. Cut the rhubarb into ½-inch pieces. Place these pieces in a large bowl, cover with 455g / 16oz of sugar and let stand for 2 hours.
2. Crush the berries and place them into a large pot. Add 455g / 16oz of sugar and stir to combine. Add the rhubarb mixture, then cook over a low heat until the sugar has dissolved.
3. Bring the mixture to a rapid boil and cook until it is thick. Test the jam by dropping a bit of jam onto a chilled saucer, popping it into a freezer for a minute, removing it and pushing the jam with your finger. If it is set, the jam will wrinkle when it is pushed. If not, cook it gently for a few more minutes and then re-test.
4. Pour the jam the into clean hot jars. Wipe the top of each jar with a clean wet cloth to remove any splatters. If you are using lids, place them in a saucepan with boiling water, boil for 1 minute and then place onto the jars. Tighten the lids and leave to rest. The jars should make a popping sound as they seal.

Store in a dark, cool place.